HOW TO ATTRACT
THE LIFE
YOU WANT

"Give me a stock clerk with a goal and I'll give you a man who will make history but give me a man without a goal and I'll give you a stock clerk"

J.C. Penney

HOW TO ATTRACT THE LIFE YOU WANT

Learn a New Way of Thinking

By Rene & Raluca Bastarache

INTRODUCTION

Have you ever wished you could feel better simply because you wanted to?

Have you ever wished you could change your financial status just by desiring it?

Have you ever wished you could become better in "any" area of your life, immediately, rather than having to wait months or years for it to happen?

Then Welcome *How to Attract the Life You Want* and consider your wish granted!

In it you'll learn about a process called the *Thought Transplant*. This isn't a surgical procedure and it doesn't require you taking any pills or health insurance.

It's a process of replacing your present way of thinking that you've grown accustomed to with a *new* or *different* way of thinking that will change you in ways you've never thought possible.

One of the definitions of insanity is: "To continue to do or think the same things over and over but expect different results."

If you continue to doing the same things that you've been doing you'll always get the same results. In order to have different results you'll need to begin thinking differently. In other words if your present way of thinking hasn't given you everything you deserve in life such as health, wealth, great relationships and happiness by now then don't you think it's time to try something different? What's required is "change".

This book will show you that change is entirely possible but it's not as easy as you may think. Otherwise you would have done it by now. Change requires doing things differently, stepping outside of your comfort zone until your new way of thinking becomes second nature.

This may sound easy to you at first glance however keep in mind that it's man's primary nature to resist change even if that change is positive. This is why so many people upon starting a New Year's resolution to quit smoking, lose weight or go to the gym will only keep it up for a few days before giving up and returning to their previous behavior.

It's easier to stay the same. It's easier to make excuses rationalizing why you failed so you can make yourself feel content with your lack of success. That's also why there's so many unsuccessful people in comparison to successful people in the world. Those who are successful decided to change and persevered until they attained their goals.

In fact this natural rebellion to change is so strong that even right now as you're reading this introduction you may already have begun the rationalization process of how you might not have the time to do this right now or maybe even trying to convince yourself that you'll look at it later on knowing that you really won't. It's much easier to rationalize not doing something than to take control of your life and "do it now".

So here's my advice and suggestion to you. Don't think of all the excuses of why you can't. Stop being a victim and take 100% control of your life. Do it now! You can attain anything you want in life but you'll have to do things differently than you have. It will require a change, dedication and perseverance. You're holding the instruction manual in your hand, what are you waiting for? Success is yours for the taking. Are you up to the challenge?

HOW TO USE THIS BOOK

You'll see several exercises that instruct you to STOP and complete them before going any further. It's important to stop and do them at that time. If you continue to read ahead without completing the exercises you'll have lost a great opportunity to learn key points about yourself.

Understand that each time you read something interesting you focus on that topic skimming over the next words until you come to another interesting point. That's the normal way people read. That's also why so many people keep finding something new that they've never seen before. It's not really new; it's simply that the topic just before it caught their interest and they mentally passed over the next interesting point. This is why you will have to read this book several times to have completed it just once.

Study this book, read it over and over until it becomes second nature. Write in it, highlight the key items and carry it with you. No one can remember everything they read so when you get an idea, write it down. An unwritten idea is a lost idea!

DEDICATION

*"Dedicated in loving memory of my Grandmother,
Rosilda Guay"*

1905 - 2007

In her 101 years of life she was a teacher, wife, mother, grandmother and responsible for creating five generations beyond her.

With over a century of love, life and experiences she was still able to touch the lives and hearts of others. She'll be truly missed.

AUTHOR

Rene A. Bastarache, CI
(Certified Instructor)

Author, Instructor and Fisherman

Rene Bastarache (Bass-tah-rash) was born, raised and presently resides in beautiful Biddeford, Maine in the Northeastern corner of the USA.

He's the author of over thirty-six self-help books and has taught thousands of people in over 150 countries how to change their lives by changing their thinking.

Mr. Bastarache is a Board Certified Hypnosis Practitioner, and the current Director of the American International Association of Hypnosis, AIA which is the largest Self-Help and Hypnotherapy Association Worldwide.

Rene's built a reputation as being the "How to Authority" on the mind, thought and imagination training as a result of writing his *CLINICAL HYPNOSIS Training Manual from A-Z* in 2005 that has become the definitive text in hypnotherapy and positive mental change worldwide.

He founded the world-renowned American School of Hypnosis in 1996 that since then has expanded to over 17 locations internationally.

Mr. Bastarache is available for public speaking events, group training, workshops and seminars worldwide. Rene and Raluca can be reached at: admin@ChooseHypnosis.com.

CO AUTHOR

Raluca E. Bastarache, CI
(Certified Instructor)

Co-Author, Instructor and Perfume Connoisseur

Raluca Bastarache (Bass-tah-rash) was born and raised in Iasi, Romania and currently resides in Biddeford, Maine in the Northeastern corner of the USA.

Mrs. Bastarache in addition to being co-author and researcher is a Success & Relationship Coach utilizing the Programs of Life Transformation and other methods described in this book.

She's the co-author of the "Clinical Hypnosis Training Manual from A-Z" which is the base curriculum of the American School of Hypnosis.

She's the current Director of the American School of Hypnosis in Biddeford and Portland, Maine, offering basic and clinical hypnotherapy certification.

She's on the Board of Advisors of the American International Association of Hypnosis, AIA.

Mrs. Bastarache is available for training, public speaking and personal coaching in goal setting, relationships and basic life issues worldwide.

TABLE OF CONTENTS

ICONS USED IN THIS BOOK

REMEMBER: You'll see sweet old grandma whenever it is important not to forget an important lesson or fact.

THOUGHTS: Here you'll find interesting thoughts, tips and information that will be useful to you.

TECHNICAL STUFF: This box is used for the technical, behind the scenes stuff and proof of various concepts in the book.

QUESTION: Here you will find common questions that have been asked with their responding answers.

EXERCISE: Helpful exercises have been included to assist you in attaining your goals and in understanding the various concepts described in this book

LEGAL NOTICE

The contents of this publication reflect the views of the authors and are an accumulation of information gathered throughout their years of experience in sales training, hypnotherapy and coaching. The authors are not responsible in any way, shape or form for any loss, mishap or liability caused by the utilization of any of the information within.

Rene or Raluca are not Medical or Mental Health Practitioners. Before making any health related changes or decisions you should consult with your physician.

No part of this publication may be reproduced, printed or transmitted in any way without the express written permission of the author Rene A. Bastarache.

EDITING NOTICE:

If you find typographical errors in this book, I'd like you to realize that they're here for a reason. Some people actually enjoy looking for them and we strive to please as many as possible. Thank you!

THE END

If you are committed to reading this book and beginning a new chapter in your life, then this is the end. It's the end of the old you. With every ending there's a new beginning. I'd like to congratulate you in advanced for taking your first step. This is the beginning of a journey that will permanently change your life. It's the end of *stinking thinking* and the beginning of *unlimited possibilities*.

A Strong Desire to Succeed

A wise Monk was conducting training with his young student in the temple one day. The topic of instruction was on the importance of having a strong desire to succeed so as to attain the path of enlightenment. The young student looked at the Monk and asked, "Master, how do I know if my desire to attain my goal is strong enough?"

The wise monk then motioned for the student to come closer as he pointed to the calm surface of a large barrel of water. "Look closely into this pool of water", said the Monk to his young student. As the young man bent over to look deep inside of the barrel the Monk placed both of his hands on the back of the boys head and forcefully pushed his face deep under the water.

The young man began thrashing his arms frantically trying to escape, as he was unable to breathe. After a couple minutes of this he felt that he was sure to drown. Suddenly the Monk pulled his head out of the water, looked at him with a warm smile and said, "When your head was under water, how strong was your desire to breathe?"

"That's how strong your desire to succeed must be."

CHAPTER 1

THE PROGRAMMING
OF MAN

"You become what you think about most of the time."

Earl Nightingale

SUCCESS STATISTICS

Less than 5% of society is truly successful. How do I define success? One of the simplest definitions of success is "the act of having a good idea and working towards it". This is also known as having a goal. It's amazing to think that only about 10% of society has goals and less than half of them work towards attaining their goals. This shows why so few are truly successful in the areas of health, wealth or happiness. After all, if you don't know where you're going, how will you ever get there?

Many feel that the reason for this low percentage of successful people may be because the formula to attaining success is some kind of elusive secret that only the elite are aware of and has been held back from us by our leaders as a way of keeping us subdued as their followers. A second possibility that is quite popular is that we're too busy living the routines of our daily lives to actually plan them. A third reason is that many people aren't aware of how to choose goals or even what to ask for. They've never been taught how to be truly successful by their parents.

Possibly one of these theories is true or maybe even all three but the fact still remains that less than 5% of society are truly successful. This helps us to understand why approximately 97% of the money in this country is controlled by only 1% of the public.

Less than 10% of society has goals.
5% of them have clear defined goals.
2% will actually act upon their goals.
1% will follow through with their goals.

The purpose of this chapter is not to impress you with statistics but to help you to understand why these statistics are so. Let's refer back to the second paragraph on this page. I'd like to suggest that the reason that most people aren't living their dream or attaining the highest possible success they're capable of is due to the manner in which they were raised. Much of it can be attributed to their caretakers and environment.

As much as we'd all like to think that our parents were perfect in every way, the bare facts are that they didn't have all of the knowledge to teach you as a child that you needed to attain your full potential. They brought you up the same way that they were brought up and very similar to the way everyone else around them was bringing up their children. The reason for this is that we live in a world of appearances. We live in a world where people follow other people. It's as if we have been conditioned to follow the group.

HOW YOU BECAME WHO YOU ARE

As a baby you were brought up by your caretakers pretty much in the same manner as every other child in your environment. You were fed, loved and clothed the best your parents knew how. You were taught the same type of lessons and information as other children in preparation to enter school.

Once you were old enough to go to school, you so desperately wanted to fit in that you decided to act like the other children there. The last thing that you wanted to do was to act in a different way that would draw attention or ridicule to you. It was very important that you fit into the mold of what was known as normal and were accepted by as many as possible. You may have even fallen into one of the group categories of being a jock, geek, nerd, greaser, cheerleader or whatever other groups existed. That category stuck with you most of your school years even if you didn't feel like you were part of it. If you had friends that were in a certain group, you were also linked to it through association.

Upon becoming an adult you decided to either go to college or to stay home and get a job. If most of your friends went to college then most likely you went too. You wanted to go to the same ones that they went to. Many went on to college even if they had no idea what they wanted to study or become. It was the thing to do. Upon graduation you hopefully got a job in your field or you took the first job you could find in order to begin paying back those huge student loans. It's amazing how many hamburger flippers have masters' degrees.

If you decided to stay home, like most people you filled out many applications and took the first job that was offered to you. When you started your job, you observed how others around you performed theirs so you could copy their behavior and do your job properly. You made friends with the people you worked with and in your free time joined in many of the same activities that they enjoyed.

You continued living this way, following others in virtually everything you did day after day. You may have gotten married, had children and found yourself raising them in the very same manner. In fact you may have found that many of your mannerisms or habits when relating to your spouse and children were similar to your own parents when they raised you. Most of your downtime was taken up by conducting mindless chores around the house and watching television that according to statistics encompassed about 25% of your free time.

At the end of your daily routine you realized that it was finally time to go to bed so you could get up in the morning to get your children off to school and start your job again the next day. This monotonous cycle went on day after day and year after year until you either retired or died.

Many people are so caught up in this type of life that they don't even realize that there is another way. After all, according to their gauge of success if their lives were very similar to their neighbors and friends then it must be good. In other words if this is all you know then this is all you'll get. Why? Because of a secret that is as old as time itself. "You become what you think about most of the time."

> **NOTE:** Now that you see how you became who you are, let's take some time to learn about the mechanics of this process. In addition to following the group, there was also much programming that took place internally. Understanding this programming that still exist and is occurring even today is the first step in creating the new you that you'd like to be.

BLUEPRINT OF BIRTH

Here you are, a newborn baby taking your first breaths in an exciting world of opportunity. You were born in a healthy, happy and orderly state. You're perfection in human form, pure potential. You have all of the same opportunities or tools to work with as anyone else born into this existence. You're the center of your universe. *Your entire "reality" revolves around you.* This is the true state of being that you were meant to experience. This is your blueprint of birth.

You have no inhibitions or restrictions. You express all of your feelings, wants and desires openly, without fear. Everything other than this, anything that doesn't conform to this orderly, perfect state of being is learned propaganda. Anything that has been learned can be unlearned. You can return to your initial blueprint. It's your "birthright" to be happy, wealthy and healthy. That's the natural state that you were ordained to be in throughout your life. That's the order of, or nature of Humanity. Anything other or contrary to this orderly state is considered a dis-order.

Orderly State of Being:

The following are in harmony with your blueprint of birth and are the natural, orderly state for humans to remain in throughout their lives. This is your birthright and anything in opposition does not exist in an orderly state.

Health	Happiness	Comfort
Security	Laughter	Wealth
Contentment	Love	Creativity

Disorderly State of Being:

The following are a threat to health and happiness and are not natural traits. They're learned behaviors that must not be accepted or chosen to take root in your programming.

Sickness	Jealousy	Anger
Disease	Greed	Guilt
Depression	Poverty	Sadness

A BRAND NEW COMPUTER CHILD

You can compare the state of mind of this newborn child with a brand-new computer that has just been taken out of its packaging. It's presently a blank slate and waiting to be programmed. It has the ability to do anything that any other computer of its type can do. What will set it apart from all other computers as time goes on will be the actual programming it receives from the outside environment otherwise known as *the programmer*.

McAflea Virus Scan
--for the Human Computer Only--

When malicious or harmful outside programming attacks a computer it is found and either eliminated or quarantined if the computer has an updated *virus scan program*. Why is this important? The negative items are not in harmony with the proper operation of the computer. A computer can be scanned for such negative programming and if too much negativity or damage has occurred it can be reformatted back to its factory or new specifications.

Anything that's in opposition to health or happiness isn't in harmony with your programming or blueprint of birth. You must be ever vigilant, constantly scanning to eliminate threatening outside input. Even if you feel that the negative programming has permeated too deeply to be corrected, just like a computer you too can also be reformatted or reprogrammed. Consider this book *your instruction manual* to return you to your initial factory specifications. Similar to any other computer manual however, reading it isn't enough. It must be studied and followed to the letter in order to be effective in making you operational once again.

THE PROGRAMMING BEGINS

Since you have no frame of reference at birth to compare anything with, every bit of input that you come in contact with you absorb like a sponge. You make no judgments as of yet and are equally as excited to learn about anything whether it be good or bad, right or wrong. Judgments will not come until you've assimilated enough information to develop your personal likes and dislikes.

As time goes on you begin to develop personal preferences that give you a frame of reference and now you begin to make personal judgments. Now your conscious mind is being developed and is screening all information so it can challenge or reject anything that you don't like. That's the purpose of the conscious mind.

As you progress you begin to form attachments and bonds to family members and others in your outside world. With these attachments you begin to learn from, depend on and trust these people and virtually anyone else you come in contact with from your environment. With this influx of information you now are able to begin to develop personal likes and dislikes. You begin to accept the belief systems of those who are responsible for your upbringing due to the repetitious nature of observation. In many cases you'll also be programmed with the same limitations, shortcomings, prejudices, traits and belief systems as your parents or guardians.

Anything you observe or learn over a period of time eventually becomes a habit through repetition and is permanently stored in your subconscious mind as individual programs. As you develop more of these programs you begin to develop your personality. These programs are what you use as reference guides to make your daily choices.

As you get older, in addition to learning and developing new programs through observation you begin to learn from teachers, friends, relatives, clergy, television, radio and by personal experiences. You're now being programmed by the bombardment of the continuous suggestions you come in contact with from virtually every direction throughout your entire waking state. You're being programmed as a result of making choices as well as not making choices in which case the programming is created by default.

That perfect child that you were just a short while ago, that had no restrictions and was full of possibilities has begun its process of conditioning. It's as if your blueprint of birth is being chiseled away bit by bit. No one is born with restrictions, fear, stress, doubt or depression. There's no such thing as a born "victim". Being a victim is a game that we play. It is a choice.

Now you're an adult. As an adult you've developed programs for virtually every situation. Throughout your day these programs are triggered or referred to through association each time you're given new stimuli in order to know how to act. You see something happening within your senses and immediately are able to associate it with an experience from your past. This's why several people can see the same thing such as an apple and have entirely different feelings about it. One may be totally delighted as it's associated with a stored program of mom's delicious apple pie cooling off on the windowsill. Another may be completely disgusted because it's associated with the program of an apple that was eaten as a child that had a worm in it and still another one may be associated with spending so much time in New York City, also known as the "Big Apple". In all three cases the apple was not seen for what it was but for the effect from the association it had from each individuals past.

ARE WE ROBOTS?

With this marvelous ability of storing these programs we're very similar to the advanced robots that you see in the science fiction movies. Every time information is fed into our neural net it's examined and associated with a stored program for a response. This process can be simply described as:

Stimuli - Examine /Associate - Response

Most people at this point are able to rely on their accumulation of programs to run their entire lives. They become so busy with their lives that they begin to settle into monotonous routines or cycles. Getting up day after day to do the same things and never questioning why they're doing them. It's as if their lives have become a programmed behavior. They begin to become victims of their own creation or of their environment. They feel like they have no choices as all of the programs they've created thus far tell them to continue doing the same things. Many become dissatisfied and stressed which perpetuates this behavior even more. They become stuck in their life cycle and feel that there's no way out.

Even though we all have the same opportunity to choose, most have allowed these choices to be made for them by society or their environment. Even their thoughts have become programmed according to appearances instead of truth. Rather than thinking of what they really want in life they focus on what they see around them thereby attracting more of it.

- They focus on the mediocrity around them and therefore attract it into their life.
- They focus on the sickness around them and become sick.
- They focus on poverty and attract it.
- They see the living conditions of those around them and attract the same.
- They see the attitudes of others and seem to develop the same ones.

This explains why most people will earn within a few thousand dollars of the same income as their group of peers. You'll notice that people who live in a middle class neighborhood will usually settle into becoming middle class with a similar type house, vehicle and lifestyle as their environment. Just think of those who constantly associate with angry people. Are they usually happy or angry? You'll see this in almost every aspect of life such as health, wealth, relationships and overall happiness.

QUESTION: Why do only a select few stand on their own by making proper choices while the majority gets stuck in cycles?

Why are some people always successful at whatever they do?

Why do some people "never" get sick?

Why are some people "always" happy?

Why? - For one reason only!

They "think and act" differently than you do.

They have developed an entirely different way of thinking and acting that gives them everything they want in life.

No one has ever taught you the proper way to think so you presently think as you were taught or observed. You have been thinking according to "observation or appearances" rather than desire.

You must re-learn the way to think properly.

We "all" were born with the same opportunities.

We "all" began in the same state of pure potential.

We "all" were destined to be, do or have whatever we wanted but when our "individual programming" began, only *a select few* where programmed to "think and act in this unique way". The majority were programmed to be the robots that "react to appearances" rather than act according to desire".

The good news!

It's not too late. You can be re-programmed and fed the correct information to think properly. You can change your life to be, have or attain anything you desire. It's your birthright.

The bad news!

It won't be easy…
It will take a commitment…
It will take practice…

> *"To think according to appearance is easy;*
> *to think truth regardless of appearances is not.*
> *It requires more effort than any other work you can do.*
> *There is no job from which most people shy away from*
> *as sustained and consecutive thought."*
>
> Wallace Wattles

You must be programmed to be "different" than you are now if you wish to change, otherwise you'll remain the "same".

THE COMMITTMENT

Before you jump in blindly and make the statement, "Oh that's easy, let's do it!" think about this for a moment… When I say you'll be different than you are now, I really mean it! This is where the commitment comes in. Just for a moment I'd like you to use your imagination:

Imagine yourself right now the way you are…
Now imagine that your facial expressions and mannerisms are completely different...
Imagine that you're alert and much more energized…

Imagine that your body is looking different but in a positive way...
Imagine that you have an entirely different personality...
You no longer like the same sports, hobbies or pastimes as before...
Even the foods you eat are different...
Imagine that you have new friends and most of your old ones think that you're strange, different and aren't comfortable being around you anymore...

Imagine that you now have a new job, a new place to live and very different goals...

This is what I mean by being different. If you commit to following this process of letting go of appearances by "practicing Elite Thought" or what we call *going through a thought transplant* you'll become a *different person* as just mentioned.

"A Thought Transplant"

Your thoughts, desires, appearance, attitude and virtually everything else about you will be different. As a bare minimum, you'll never look at things the same way again.

Once you begin to think differently, you'll become "different", not the same, other than you are, unfamiliar, are you getting the picture? If you were to remain the same, nothing would change. In order to change you must be different. There must be a change.

Think of it as installing a new operating system in your computer. It's the same computer but it now works completely different. Is it worth it? For those who have made the change already, they would all say an astounding "yes!" In order to make this change from where you are now, to being happy, healthy or wealthy, it does take a commitment. It will not happen overnight but it doesn't need to be a long drawn out affair either. It can be quick according to your efforts.

It's a process that takes practice and perseverance. How long must you commit? Until you've attained it!

So are you still willing and anxious to commit to this process? If you answered yes, then congratulations to you. Take a moment to celebrate your new life and say goodbye to the old one!

Now, let's get to work...

SUGGESTIONS ARE EVERYWHERE

You're being conditioned through some form of suggestion the majority of each day.

> **DEFINITION:** Suggestion - is defined as: *the process by which a physical or mental state is influenced by a thought or idea (the power of suggestion).*
>
> Merriam-Webster's Dictionary

You're either open to suggestion or resisting suggestion constantly, there's no halfway. It may be positive or negative conditioning. That's the entire purpose of advertising. To entice you to choose one product over another or to slant you towards thinking a certain way that will be advantageous to the advertiser in some manner. It happens to you whether you like it or not, or whether you want it to or not. But there is something that you can do about it.

Suggestions are being delivered to you directly, indirectly, covertly, subliminally and every other way you can imagine on a continual basis. They're coming to you from your computer, magazines, billboards, newspapers, radio, television, at the cinema, on the phone, driving down the street, in the supermarket or other stores, at school, church, from the government, on vacation, restaurants, the gym, at sports, meetings, work, from your children, parents, spouse, friends, non-friends, co-workers, clergy, teachers, mentors and even your pets.

Hopefully now you are beginning to see the scope of this. They're all taking part in your daily conditioning and building of programs. The same programs that are turning you into the person you are now and the person you are becoming.

Our purpose of teaching you this is not to eliminate what's happening to you. It's to create awareness so you may be able to take control of your future conditioning. This will give you the opportunity to act or make choices rather that allowing it to control you.

SIXTEEN WAYS WE'RE BEING CONDITIONED THROUGH SUGGESTIONS EVERYDAY

Here's the listing of just sixteen of the many ways most people are being conditioned through powerful suggestion each day. While reading them, see how many resonate with you.

1. **Signs, advertising, logos and marketing gimmicks are everywhere.**

You're continually being bombarded with suggestions to act now and purchase products from television, radio, junk mail, newspapers, store window ads, magazines, department stores and supermarkets just to name a few. There's virtually no place you can go where you're not in contact with some form of advertising suggestion.

Many successful Real Estate agents when conducting Open Houses will turn on every light in the house and burn a candle with the scent of apple pie as a way of enticing customers. The reason for this is so when the customer enters the house and smells the apple pie scent it's immediately associated with mom's home cooked apple pie, cooling on the windowsill, from when they were children. The association of a bright happy home with mom's cooking is very suggestible to the client and favorable to the possible sale.

2. **Shopping at the grocery store.**

This can be a battle of resisting suggestion. Some stores even have demonstrators trying to tempt you with free samples. The scent of freshly baked goods being prepared in the bakery... Attractive signage and inviting music in the background... Sales displays of *easy to prepare* meals right at eye level and the list goes on. Think of the many times you went into the grocery store to buy only four products but came out with fifteen.

3. Everything happening at once.

Known as the *confusional method* or *bypassing critical mass.* Similar to doing your taxes while someone is having a conversation with you at the same time. If you're focusing on your taxes, everything in the conversation is being absorbed by the subconscious mind like a sponge. This is why it's detrimental to have the television or radio on while working, eating or sleeping.

People who are extreme multi-taskers experience this. They attain a brainwave level in the High Beta range, which is known as critical mass. At this point they're very open and susceptible to suggestions as their resistance to outside input is almost non-existent.

4. Daydreaming in classrooms or work.

Daydreaming is a hypnotic state that's much deeper than most people would think. It's actually the same level of hypnosis that you would be in for painless childbirth or to have dental work done without anesthesia. The daydreaming state is dominated by your imagination and is accompanied by a state of amnesia. This is why when you're daydreaming in class you don't remember what was being said and may even have a feeling of lost time.

5. Fear of deadlines or loss.

You may have heard the slogan before that fear's a great motivator. Fear's also a powerful tool utilized in the acceptance of suggestion. It's now and has been successfully used in virtually every walk of life such as sales, government, religion, family, school, work and countless other areas.

"Call now, we only have two left on hand or the sale ends tomorrow."

"Keep the noise down in your room or you'll be punished."

"Meet the 12:00 deadline or you're fired!"

"Buy the best security system or your house will be broken into."

"Call your doctor now, before something happens to you."

6. Music controls the mood.

Music is extremely hypnotic. The effect of music can cause you to become extremely relaxed one moment and very agitated the next. Both are favorable for accepting suggestions without resistance.

You'll see a huge difference between the behavior and attitudes of people who frequently listen to classical music in compared to those who listen to the more aggressive music available today. The same can be said for the difference between the children whose parents prefer them to watch G-rated Disney cartoons in comparison to violent and destructive cartoons.

The words or messages that are in music can have an overwhelming effect on people as well. Some of the older Country Western songs for instance can really bring you down if you listen to the lyrics. Many seem to focus on the tragedies or hard-times in life. We sometime joke about how may tragedies can be put into one song such as a country singer singing of how his wife left him for a traveling salesman. She secretly snuck out in the middle of the night with his dog and drove away in his brand new pickup truck. Now he's left with nothing but his old shotgun, drinking a bottle of Jack Daniels, sitting in his trailer. Listening to a song like that can bring on depression.

Placebo, the sugar pill effect.

A placebo is a non-effective substance or object given to someone by a person who is in authority (doctor, minister, parent, boss or supervisor) leading the person to believe that it will cure or solve his or her situation. Any effect that this placebo has is based on the power of suggestion.

An example would be; if you were given sugar pills by your doctor thinking that they were an asthma cure and within a few months your asthma improved. Approximately 1/3rd of the medications prescribed today for various disorders utilize the placebo effect. As long as there's a belief that it will work, a hope of being cured and someone in authority such as a doctor to say it will; most of the elements of a placebo recovery are there.

8. Nocebo, the sugar pill side effect.

A Nocebo is also based upon the power of suggestion. Going back to the example of the placebo pills; a nocebo would be experiencing the same reaction of side effects from the placebo as if it were the actual pills. It's all of the negative placebo effects.

9. Propaganda. *(Anything that is taught with a motive or preference)*

Propaganda is a strong form of suggestion that's used continually in the areas of religion, employment, sales, government, education, sports and even sexual preference. Often times these suggestions cause rivalry, fierce competition and even wars.

Your company develops the best Widgets available on the market.

Your football team is superior to any other team.

Everyone in your country is wonderful, everyone in the neighboring country are terrorist.

This company will save me hundreds of dollars over that company. After all, I heard it on television!

10. Relaxation.

This is probably the most well known vehicle of suggestibility today. It's used quite extensively in the mental health and medical fields to increase suggestibility. It's the basis of meditation and guided imagery. Even parents use these techniques with their children by telling them to take a deep breath to get them to calm down. Once you're relaxed, positive suggestions can easily be given and accepted.

Many companies have also associated their products so as to *group them* mentally with suggestions of relaxation to sell them, such as coffee, cigarettes, luxury automobiles, furniture, chocolate and vacations. The added suggestion or conditioning of relaxation makes the item more appealing even if it's not so.

11. Tell me a story.

Storytelling can be a very effective form of delivering suggestion by having embedded messages or metaphors included within them. This is most often seen in the writing of fairytales, nursery rhymes, fables and parables.

- Being told stories by your parents to get you to conform. One would be reading the story, "The Boy who Cried Wolf" to a child who has a problem with lying.

- Reading bedtime stories that include a *moral* to your children. This helps them to associate with the way things should be in a perfect world.

- Beginning a church sermon or a corporate talk with a story or joke with a message in it. People relate to stories of other people who have overcome similar problems to theirs. It can eliminate the rebelliousness of being confronted directly with their own issues.

12. Reading is magic.

Reading stories with suggestive messages such as in telling a story like in the previous section is also very suggestive to the reader. Since suggestions are being delivered as you read it's a form of self-hypnosis. In fact, reading anything from magazines, newspapers, web pages, articles or virtually anything you read that has been written for the purposes of soliciting some form of suggestion or desired response has this effect.

> **TIP:** It is important to note that if you are reading a story to a child as a means of giving them positive suggestions for change, keep in mind that unless you are actively resisting the suggestions you are reading, you are being conditioned as well. All suggestion is self-suggestion!

13. Writing.

I've found that just about any self-help course or program will encourage you to "write down" your goals on paper. Writing something down will give you a fairly complete concept of what you want. Then the act of forming the letters as you write engrains the suggestion even more.

For years in schools, students were made to write things on the blackboard repetitively in order to get them to remember or learn a lesson. Writing has a way of imprinting suggestions in your mind more than reading, typing or recording. If you write it, you can see it.

14. Repetition, how does it affect you?

Anything that is repeated continually for a minimum of approximately 21 days becomes a habit. Once it becomes a habit it seems to work on automatic pilot. This happens without even having to think about the process anymore. Here are some examples:

Reciting the alphabet
Typing on the keyboard
Answering the phone
Driving to work each day
Brushing your teeth

Each morning when you get up you have a brand new day in front of you. You have the same opportunity as anyone else to be original, do something spectacular or spontaneous. Even with this new day in front of them, most people will do the very same thing that they did the day before. They've created a routine, especially during the workdays. Even something like changing the time of their coffee break or taking a different route to work can seem like the biggest inconvenience.

This same repetition method is used in creating faith or belief through the propaganda of various organizations such as schools, governments or religions. The process of repetition creates faith, then habit and then belief. It's an actual scientific process occurring within the neural connections of the brain, which we'll explain thoroughly in a future chapter.

15. Resisting suggestions.

If you become aware that you're being given suggestions and immediately resist by giving yourself counter suggestions *(opposing ideas or thoughts)* you're still in a state of suggestibility since you accepted the counter or opposing suggestion from yourself. When you reject or replace any suggestion you are still accepting its alternative.

16. Pygmalion effect

This is more commonly known as the *teacher-expectancy effect* and it refers to situations in which some students perform better than others simply because they were expected to. If a group of students were treated as if they were smarter than another group for whatever reason, they would react more favorably than those treated in the opposite manner. It's a sort of self-fulfilling prophecy.

Tests of this phenomenon have been conducted by separating students into groups according to the color of their eyes. On one day the blue-eyed students were told they were smarter and superior to their brown-eyed counterparts. Upon being tested they scored considerably higher. A few days later the brown-eyed group was told they were the smarter ones and they scored higher than the blue-eyed group. The effect of teachers, parents, or whoever's in a position of authority has a huge effect on their followers.

This effect is also used by parents that favor one child over another. If the parents refer to one child as intelligent and the other as below average in most cases the children will grow into those categories. If a child is continually told that he or she is uncontrollable, unhealthy or unreliable the child will usually fulfill the parents' expectation.

These are just sixteen of the many ways you're being conditioned each day. There are many more that can be listed but we have enough here for you to understand what's happening. It's not something that just happens to other people in far off places, it's happening to "you" right now. It's staggering to see how much of our lives are actually being controlled by outside sources.

As mentioned earlier, awareness that this constant conditioning is happening is just the first step in understanding. Programming is continually being added even now to your subconscious storage by your environment. It's a never-ending occurrence, but you can be in control of your programming rather than being a victim of it.

DISTORTED IMAGES

In addition to learning how to change your thought process it's also important to change the way you look at

yourself. Your self-image has become distorted through years of conditioning; similar to the image you see when you look into a carnival mirror. You're not seeing what is actually there.

When you look in the mirror, the person that you're seeing isn't who you are now. You're seeing the result of your past experiences and memories. You're in actuality a shadow of your past. If your memories or experiences of the past made you who you are now then your present memories and experiences are making you who you'll be. You'll create this "new you" through your corrected thought process.

Here's an important truth that is *vital* to understand about your mind...

> *"The subconscious mind does not understand the difference between an imagined memory or a real one."*

They hold the same value and importance. This is how you'll create new memories to replace the old ones. Through the use of your imagination and repetition you'll begin the reprogramming process of building the new you.

You're still that perfect being that you were at birth. Your blueprint has not been lost. You have the ability to return yourself to that blueprint of truth, health and happiness. You'll soon be able to look in the mirror and see a true reflection of the remarkable being that you really are. We'll show you how.

> *"In the journey of self-improvement the difficulty isn't in finding the instructions, it's in following them."*

THE GOLDEN BUDDHA

In Bangkok Thailand there is a place called the Temple of the Golden Buddha. The Buddha that sets in the middle of this temple has a very interesting history and it is also made of solid gold.

Approximately 900 years ago when the Burmese were about to attack the city of Ayutthaya, the monks there were afraid that the Burmese would steal their golden statue so they decided to cover it with about ten inches of clay. This was actually what most of the Buddha statues were made of in that time so covering this statue with clay would raise no attention. As a result of the attack the statue had not been noticed by the Burmese military however they did kill all of the monks thereby leaving no survivors to tell the story of how there was a Golden Buddha secretly hidden under the clay.

Two centuries later in 1957 the statue was being moved in a wooden crate to a new temple in Bangkok. It was thought to have very little worth. Upon arrival the workmen who were moving it with a large crane lowered it and left it in the mud to finish the move in the morning since it was raining and getting dark. The crate was covered with plastic tarps for the evening. Early the next morning one of the monks upon examining the condition of the statue noticed that there was a crack in its surface. Looking into the crack in the clay with a lantern he noticed what appeared to be something yellow and shining. He called the other monks and they began to remove the clay carefully to discover that the statue was made of pure gold.

You are very similar to the statue. You are perfection inside. Everything you need to attain your goals of health, wealth, relationships or happiness is already there. It has simply been covered with years of conditioning, experiences and decisions (clay). In order to get back to the perfection inside, you simply need to chisel off the clay. It is a matter of digging through the negative conditioning and experiences of your life so you can uncover the true you.

THE PURPOSE OF LIFE

What's the purpose of life? That's a question that mankind has been asking since the beginning of time. I'd like to say that I have the answer but if I actually did have the answer that would be sure to cause lots of controversy. People would say to themselves, "Who does this guy think he is to have the answer that men have been searching for since the beginning of time? Is he that arrogant and full of himself that he really thinks he has the answer?" Don't worry, I don't really "think" I have the answer because I actually "do" have the answer, and I'm even going to share it with you right now.

My theory on the purpose of life can be summed up in two words and those two words are:

"Be happy"

Think about that for a moment, the purpose of life is simply to be happy. Isn't that a wonderful concept? Did you expect more? Some people feel that we were predestined to come to this earth and have a journey to complete. Some feel that they must live meager lives or live as hermits. Some feel that they are here to atone for the mistakes of a previous life. Some people even feel that we are on this earth to create experiences to be used as entertainment in the afterlife.

THOUGHTS: There are probably enough theories of why we are here to be able to write a complete book however I think it is safe to assume that being happy does not go against any one of them. One of my favorite sayings that I heard years ago is, "Man is that he might have joy."

If we actually are all connected somehow, through spirit, energy, matter or as the immortal Albert Einstein had theorized many years ago in his E theory that we are all part of a vast, vibrating sea of energy;

wouldn't the whole concept of *being happy* affect everyone? Not only does happiness feel good but it's also very contagious.

Happiness has been known to heal and to alleviate harmful afflictions such as stress, fear, anxiety, depression, loneliness, anger and even sadness. Many of these things are known to be major factors in the developing of sickness and disease.

THE UNIVERSAL PLAN

Does the Universe have a plan? Does it have a purpose, a function? Actually it does. The purpose of the Universe is to increase, expand, grow and to constantly become more than it is. In fact, that is one constant that can be found in everything. According to the Universe there is no bad or good, right or wrong, those concepts are man-made. So growth can be either positive or negative as long as it is able to become more.

One of the strongest instincts of man and all living creatures is to reproduce. This instinct has been a prevalent topic that has been studied, debated, sung about and extensively written of since primitive man to the current day. Man's extremely driven to reproduce. He teaches nurtures and protects his young. In some societies these family units will stay together for as long as three to four generations under the same roof.

Animals also have this instinct as many of them will reproduce and even pair up with the same mate for life. Animals are also very protective of their families and in many instances have even sacrificed themselves to ensure the safety and growth of their young ones.

You can see this same instinct prevalent in insects, fish and even plants. Plants grow, flower, turn to seed and then germinate so they can multiply and grow in larger numbers. Everything increases.

We as human beings want more of everything "good" that we have. In fact we even want more of the good things that we don't have as well. It's human nature to want increased health, better relationships, better jobs, improved living conditions, more wealth, more happiness, more laughter, longer lives and even more time. Everything that we have that's good, we want more.

ALIGNMENT WITH SOURCE

If the nature of the Universe or Source is to grow and constantly be more then having more of whatever we want is in harmony with Source. So to have more of anything such as health, wealth or happiness is in keeping with the alignment or commandments of the Universe, Source or God. Having less resulting in being destitute, struggling, sickly, depressed, unhappy or in bad relationships must obviously not be in alignment. It's in opposition of the very nature of the Universe as well as the purpose of life. It's contrary to growth.

It's amazing to see how some people say it's wrong or against the desires of God to have riches or the finer things in life. They feel they should live a meager or destitute life of suffering to gain his favor. This is so far from the truth as even the leaders of the largest religious organizations today live in comfort, drive beautiful luxury cars and meet in buildings that would rival the temples of King Solomon. So in living a life of squalor, in addition to being out of alignment or favor with the Divine they're only hurting or depriving themselves.

By having more of everything, in addition to growing you have the ability to help so many more to grow. You can teach others by example how to be healthy and happy. Aspiring to be healthy, wealthy and happy is the most divine of goals. If you're engaged in this endeavor you're in harmony with the Universe and it will in turn assist you in ways that you cannot yet imagine. Being in harmony or in sync with the Universe or Source energy will only bring you more abundance. It's the only thing that can happen. Being out of alignment will only bring you more lack and misery.

"Here is the formula to success in all things. Align your goals with the universal purpose of increasing your life as well as the lives of others. Be of service to others and by doing so you will receive rewards from the universe beyond your desires."

Wallace Wattles

Let's break this concept down a little further. Take a moment to think of some of the wealthiest people you know. What do they do for a living? You may have on your list people who sing, act or even do public speaking. Those are all forms of service. They entertain people, they teach people, they help people to be happy and lead more fulfilling lives. They're assisting in this universal mission of expansion. Since they're being of service they're being rewarded for their service. You can add to this list, business owners, stockbrokers, politicians, computer moguls, talk show host and the list goes on and on. It seems like those that help the public the most are the ones who are doing the best.

"Success leaves behind clues."

THOUGHTS: There are enough clues to prove this concept all around you as well as every day in the newspapers and on television. If you want to be successful, help others to be successful. Do something that will effect, enhance or progress the lives of others. If you want to be happy, help others to be happy.

NON-ALIGNMENT WITH SOURCE

When you're not in alignment with this universal purpose there's struggle, difficulty and disorder in your life. Take a moment to think of all the people you know who don't serve others in any way. Think about the people who are concerned only for themselves and don't contribute to society. Those people who feel that society, the government or even their family owes them a living. Even though they're able to contribute physically and mentally they decide to do nothing. In comparison to the first group that you thought of, where do these people stand? You may find that many of them are broken down, sickly, depressed, destitute or even worse.

It's amazing to notice the amount of people who after retiring and decide to just sit home and relax, suddenly become sickly and often times die within a short period of time. However those who retire and continue to be of service to others seem to remain healthy and lead long fulfilling lives. There are many ways to be of service, which don't require full-time employment. Even being able to give advice to others is being of service.

"The Universe rewards those who are actively engaged in its purpose of increase with added health, wealth, happiness and longevity."

GODS PLAN

How does this Universal Plan compare with God's Plan? Are they in alignment? In the Old Testament, specifically in the book of Genesis man is commanded to be fruitful and multiply.

"And God said unto them, Be fruitful, and multiply, and replenish the earth, and subdue it: and have dominion over the fish of the sea, and over the fowl of the air, and over every living thing that moveth upon the earth." Genesis 1:28

That statement seems to be pretty clear and to the point. We're commanded to expand, to improve and be more than what we are. This can also be seen in the New Testament as it is spoken of in the *parable of the talents*. This parable speaks of making the best with what you're given. It speaks of investing what you have in order to receive more rather than simply holding onto what you have or hiding it to keep it safe. In countless instances throughout the Bible you'll hear commands, pleas and requests to love one another, help one another and give to each other. Service seems to be a major theme throughout its teachings.

This concept of growth through self-increase and service can be found through the teachings of virtually every faith and philosophy on the face of this earth. Read the following statements and see if you've ever heard any of them before:

"If you want to learn something well, teach it."

"If you want to be truly wealthy, help others to attain wealth."

"In order to have a friend, be a friend."

"Give a man a fish and he will eat for a day, teach him to fish and he'll eat forever."

"Wherever two or more are gathered in my name, there I am."

REMEMBER:

1. Everyone was born with the same tools and the same opportunities for greatness.

2. Your blueprint of birth is one of health, wealth and happiness. Anything other than that is a disorder.

3. Any disorder can be returned to order by following the procedures set out in this book.

4. Your parents were not prepared to raise you according to your true potential.

5. You were raised the same way most of those in your community were raised.

6. Most people are too busy living their lives to plan their lives.

7. You're being conditioned constantly through suggestion every day.

8. Most people have a very distorted self-image.

9. The purpose of life is to be happy.

10. The Universal purpose is to expand.

11. If you can align yourself with the Universe, all will be well.

CHAPTER 2

FROM THREE MINDS
TO MATTER

*"Whether you think you can or you can't,
either way you are right."*

Henry Ford

THE HUMAN MIND

The mind is much more than an organ, it's an elaborate system comprised of many parts, each with separate but equally important functions. For our purposes, we'll breakdown the brain into three categories. They're the conscious, the subconscious and the superconscious minds.

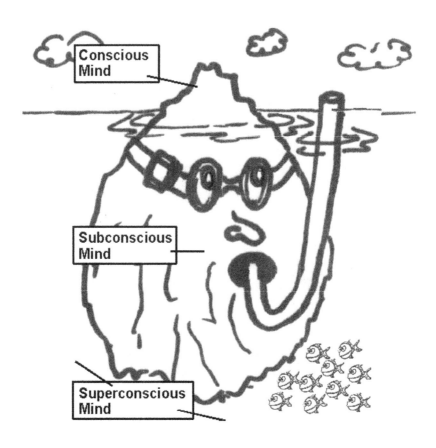

CONSCIOUS - THE VISIBLE MIND

There's a difference between the brain and the mind. The brain's the physical organ and the mind's the unseen animation of thought and storage. Sometimes we call it the brainpower.

For many years it was said that we only use about 10% of our brainpower. In recent years we've found that statement not to be true. In fact we use all of it. The conscious mind however only makes up a very small portion of it. This is probably where the misconception came from. The conscious mind would be similar to the portion of the iceberg in the previous picture that's extending above the water level. Even though that's all you can see visibly, there's so much more going on that's unseen just under the surface.

1. The conscious mind is a creature of habit.

The conscious mind enjoys remaining the same. It's a creature of habit, wanting everything to stay "status quo". It doesn't like to be inconvenienced or to do anything different from what it's done in the past, even if the proposed change is a positive one and to your benefit. This's why you seem to have so much resistance to change. This is the exact reason why when someone wants to quit smoking for example they may quit for three to five days but the majority of them will go right back to smoking again or when someone's trying to lose weight and they do really great for a short while and then bounce right back to where they were before like a yo-yo.

"If you do the same things for the next five years that you did
the last five years; five years from now you will be in
the same place that you are today!"

This trait of the conscious mind is especially important to keep in mind when you're attempting to improve yourself through the instruction in this book. Many of these exercises are based on change.

They're based on doing things different than you may have done before in order to help you to improve your situation in life. This doing things different, or stretching in any way to attain more than you have is exactly what makes the conscious mind rebel.

When doing these exercises you may immediately feel resistance even though you know it's important to change. Your conscious mind will quickly begin to rationalize that maybe you're okay the way you are now. You must be aware of this trait and be prepared to deal with it when it shows its face. The good thing is that upon daily repetition this rebelliousness will become less and eventually nonexistent as you develop your new habits.

"People are anxious to improve their circumstances but are unwilling to improve themselves as it's against the nature of their conscious mind to change; therefore they remain stuck."

2.   The conscious mind is naturally negative, untrusting and suspicious.

To explain how it's geared negatively let me use this example. Imagine a person walking up to you that you've never met before who looks at you and says, "You're the most beautiful woman I've ever met." Or if you're a man, imagine this stranger saying, "You're the most intelligent person I've ever met; in fact I'd love to write a book about your intelligence."

Most people upon hearing these type of complements will step back a moment and respond with something like, "What are you trying to sell me?" or "Okay, what's going on?" Your mind immediately goes o the defensive and is waiting for the other foot to drop. Even though this stranger may have meant the complement that he gave you the conscious mind will not accept it because of its negative or protective nature.

THE FACTS: It's important to understand these traits of the conscious mind and to always be aware of them when deciding to make positive changes in your life. These two traits are what stand in your way of self-improvement.

The Conscious Mind is:

- The command center of the mind.
- It's the decision-maker.
- Focused on the five senses of sight, sound, touch, smell and taste.
- This is where your thought process begins.
- This is where you create your goals.
- This is the place of reasoning.
- It's where input is received and associated with your stored programs.
- It's the busy part of the mind that's used for math functions, studying, speaking, playing sports, acting or reacting, analysis, ego and logic.

It's the part of the mind that you're using right now to understand this book. When you're working on your computer, reading, writing, playing sports, or doing any other type of busy activity you're utilizing your conscious mind.

SUBCONSCIOUS - THE UNSEEN MIND

The subconscious mind is the remainder of the mind or brainpower that doesn't include the conscious mind. Looking at the previous picture of the iceberg it would be similar to the unseen portion that lies just below the surface of the water. The visible portion may seem small and unthreatening to passing ships but the huge unseen portion under the surface has the mass, power and capability of sinking even the largest luxury liner if it ventured too close.

The purpose of the subconscious mind is simply to take in and store information. It's like a sponge where it comes to input. It acts in a manner similar to the hard drive of a computer. Everything that you experience each day is logged in your subconscious mind. It receives everything that it can through your five senses that's within its range. Whether the suggestion is positive or negative, good or bad, it accepts them all. The subconscious mind doesn't make any judgment on the input it receives. That's the purpose of the conscious mind.

Upon prolonged repetition of suggestions or associated with emotional or traumatic experiences the suggestions are permanently stored as programs to be referred to in the future. These programs cannot be eliminated; they can only be overridden with new programs but the initial programs still remain dormant.

Another feature of the subconscious mind is that it's extremely innocent and naïve. It acts very similar to a five year old child. Your subconscious mind wants to help you and certainly has the power to help you in any way that you wish. In most cases however it doesn't know the proper way to help you unless it's given detailed instructions.

Being similar to a five year old child, in addition to giving it detailed instruction it's also very helpful to give it a reward for accomplishing the task. Giving a reward isn't something to be taken lightly. Just think of yourself in the following scenario for a moment. If someone in your family were to ask you to wash a sink full of dirty dishes your response may not be too enthusiastic. However if they offered you $45.00 to do the dishes, you may look at the entire project a little differently.

FOUR RULES OF THE SUBCONSCIOUS

1. Obedience to the Conscious Mind at all Times

The subconscious mind does exactly as the conscious mind desires:
It doesn't always do exactly what the conscious mind "says" however;
many times what you say and what you desire are two different things.
It's similar to a childlike "out of control" Genie in a bottle. It will
"always" grant your wishes!

> *"Wherever you place your focus; that's what you're
> drawing to you. This is called your Point of Attraction."*

Unfortunately the conscious mind doesn't always make the best
decisions. A good example of this is the story of one of my past clients
who came to see me because he had a strong desire to pass the *Bar-
Exam* to be a lawyer. Before coming to see me he had attempted to
pass the exam on his own but had failed miserably on four separate
occasions. In our session I gave him suggestions for study habits, test
taking and enhanced memory. Finally the day of the test came and of
course he did his best. As a result of the test he failed once again but
by only *one point*.

He was actually so excited that he came this close to passing the test
that he wanted to come back to my office so we could do another
session. I mentioned to him that I felt there was a little more going on
than simply needing study habits and test taking. There seemed to be
something deeper that was holding him back from passing the test.

During our discussion I asked him what he was doing right now for
work to which he responded that he worked for the law firm doing
research and paperwork. It was a good job and he got paid very well.
Then I asked him what he would be doing if he actually passed the Bar
Exam. To that he responded that he would be still working for the
same law firm but now instead of doing research and paperwork he'd

actually be an independent attorney and responsible for bringing in his own clients. He was a bit worried about this because he doubted his ability as a salesperson and felt that if he didn't produce enough clients that he would be terminated.

From listening to his responses you may have already figured out what was going on in his mind. Remember that the subconscious mind acts similar to a five year old child. How would a five year old respond to the two options just given in the previous paragraph? He may respond by saying, "Even though I didn't pass the test yet, I do have a great job. If I do pass the test I might get fired. I think I'll fail the tests on purpose so I can be safe."

Even though my client said that he wanted to pass the Bar-Exam; subconsciously that really wasn't his desire. His desire was to have a good job. His desire was to remain the same, so that's exactly what happened. This goes to show that sometimes what you say and what you truly want are two different things. You need to take the time to examine your desires to make sure that what you want is in alignment with your actual focus and attention. Your subconscious mind will get confused with crossed signals.

> *"Sometimes what you say and what you*
> *truly want are two different things."*

THOUGHTS: Humans are ***ordering machines***. We are constantly ordering things through our thoughts either on purpose or by default. We order the things that we want and we also order the things that we don't want. This is why it is vitally important to control your thought process.

If your point of attraction is on sickness then you're attracting sickness.

If your point of attraction is on wealth then you're attracting wealth.

If you're surrounded by misery and aren't actively eliminating the thoughts of misery then misery is being attracted to you.

This process of always attracting what you focus on from moment to moment is continually happening whether you like it or not or if you believe in it or not. It's a universal constant.

The Subconscious Mind is:

- Similar to the hard drive and memory center of a computer.
- The imagery center.
- A place of creativity, dreams, abstract and emotion.
- Where recognition takes place.
- A place of meditation.
- The starting point of intuition and psychic ability.
- Where your neural connections are re-wired to create new habitual programs.
- The place where your many developed programs are stored for ongoing association.
- It's also responsible for the complete operation and upkeep of your body. It's what keeps your heart beating, blood pumping, lungs breathing, nails and hair growing and all the other functions that are necessary to keep you healthy and alive both when you're awake and sleeping.

2. Doesn't Understand Negative

The Subconscious doesn't understand negative. When you say that you don't want something, your point of attraction or focus is on what you "don't" want. The subconscious mind will always give the conscious what it asks for but sometimes there's confusion in the asking. So when you say, "I don't want to be sick." You're placing your attention on being sick and that's what you'll get more of. Instead you should say. I want to be healthy.

Here's a little test for you...

Right now... don't think of an apple!

Did you think of it? Of course you did. In order to "not" think of something, you need to focus on what "not" to think about. By telling you not to think of an apple, the first thing that popped into your mind was an apple.

This is one of the biggest reasons why people fail. *(Even Adam and Eve had problems with an apple.)* ☺ People have a tendency of saying what they *don't* want. Many times in coaching, when asking people what they want they'll usually answer with what they "don't" want instead.

"I don't want to be broke."
"I don't want to keep fighting with my spouse."
"I don't want to be sick."

With these three previous statements, what are they placing their focus on? Being broke, fighting and being sick. So the subconscious mind will respond with, "Make it so!"

3. Doesn't Understand Humor

The subconscious mind doesn't understand humor. Being similar to a five year old it will take whatever you say literally even though you may be joking. If you were watching a comedian perform who was extremely funny, and you turned to your five-year-old son and said,

"This guy really kills me!" how do you think he'd take that comment? He'd probably wonder why this comedian wants to kill you and then begin crying due to the worry of losing you.

4. Doesn't Understand Sarcasm

Remembering that you're dealing with a child mentality again, so you must be careful how you word things. There's actually no productive or positive use for sarcasm. It's simply a humorous way to hurt or insult someone. How would a five year old child understand and react to comments such as;

"That guy is a real pain in the neck."
"I'd give my right arm for a glass of water right now."
"Break a leg!"
"Stop worrying or your head's going to explode."

These statements when heard by a five-year-old would be taken literally and obviously not in the way they were intended to be taken. How do you guard against this in the future? Don't use sarcasm and speak plainly.

EFFECTS OF NEGATIVE STATEMENTS

In society today we're constantly being bombarded by outside influences that we seem to have no control over, or do we? It seems that in almost every moment of our waking day we're being influenced by outside sources just about everywhere we look. It's almost as if you can close your eyes, point your head in any direction, and when you open your eyes there's some kind of advertisement or suggestions within your view to try to influence you in some manner.

How many negative statements do you hear around you in the

course of a day? "I don't want to be like that person." "I don't want to gain weight." "I never seem to have enough money." "I always seem to lose." and the list goes on and on. In each one of these scenarios the subconscious mind will give you whatever you're placing your focus on. So in fact you're actually making the exact thing happen that you didn't want to happen.

The first key to changing this behavior is to be aware of it. By becoming aware of your own self-talk you can begin to change your life towards the positive. However, how about all the outside negative statements coming to you on a daily basis? What can be done about those? By becoming aware of everything that you hear and see on a daily basis you can begin to program yourself for health, wealth, better relationships and happiness. You're in the driver's seat and able to change your own destiny at any time.

Keep away from any negative influence as much as possible. Get away from complainers, controllers, backbiters, gossips, negative attitudes and doomists. You'll notice that when many negative people are gathered together that they can hardly wait for their turn to come up so they can tell their hardship story. This is poison to your mind and you must eliminate it. Like attracts like, so, gravitate and spend time with those people that you'd like to have similar qualities as.

STOP SHOULDING

We all seem to have our own ideas of what life should be like. Many times we find ourselves saying ...

I should be more caring.
I should be prettier or more handsome.
I should lose weight.
I should stop smoking
I should work harder.

I should make more money.
He shouldn't do that.
You shouldn't wear that.
You shouldn't say that.
You shouldn't go there.
You shouldn't drive that way.
You shouldn't be so angry.

There are more "shoulds" than you can ever imagine. By setting ourselves up with all of these "shoulds" we also feel many times that others should fall within our guidelines of how people should be. So when someone doesn't do what we think they should do we become upset. If they don't have the same morals, appreciation, understanding, or even driving skills; we tend to judge, criticize, and in many cases become stressed. It's important to eliminate the "shoulds" from our lives and to try our best to simply be who we are!

"Stop shoulding on yourself and others!"

MONITORING YOUR THOUGHTS

Now you can see the importance of monitoring your thoughts so you can say exactly what you mean. Be aware of how the subconscious mind reacts to your thought process and begin monitoring your thoughts.

Here are some additional methods that you can use that will help you to keep your thought process on the right track which will in turn attract more of what you want to your life and less of what you don't want.

1.   Thought Stopping

You're going to have thoughts every minute of every day either way whether you follow this advice or not. Knowing that … why not try to train your thoughts to be positive, motivational and happy?

How can you change negative thoughts?

Through a technique known as *thought stopping*. Before you attempt *thought stopping* it's important for you to realize that there are certain lines of thinking that are unproductive and possibly even harmful to you. These lines of thought should be stopped immediately.

The process works like this. As soon as a negative or unproductive thought enters your mind or you're thinking in a negative way, simply say to yourself out loud, "Stop!" and watch the negative thought fade away.

Even though this seems very simple, if you make a point of practicing it in your life on a regular basis you'll find it to be very helpful in your progression. Also with negative programming you can stop it in the same manner.

QUESTION: Can I say anything other than Stop?

Some other words that can be used as a substitute to "stop" are "cancel" or "delete". One additional point that is very important to the process is once you've said the word stop or cancel, you must *swap* your thinking to a different line of thought. Stopping alone is not enough; you must "Stop and Swap". That means once you've stopped the negative thought you must begin a different line of thinking to send you in a positive direction.

2. Never End a Negative Statement

When you find yourself saying something negative or unproductive, simply don't finish the sentence or end it with a positive statement.

3. Distraction

Distract yourself with something radically different. If you find yourself thinking negatively, then find something different to think about. A good example is to listen to positive uplifting music. Another is to watch a comedy on television. You may want to get up and go for a brisk walk outside. Maybe even stand up and hop on one foot. There are so many options that you can choose from depending on where you are and the situation. It's important to do something different to break the flow of negativity.

4. Eliminate the words "don't, can't, try and no."

These are all very damaging words in your speech process. Rather than using these words from now on find positive alternatives and you'll find your speech to become much more effective.

UPERCONSCIOUS - THE UNIVERSAL MIND

This part of the mind is not as well known as the conscious and subconscious. The reason for this is it does not encompass the physical or contained parts of the brain. It operates primarily in the Quantum World. It's actually outside of the brain in the realm of thought. It's the connecting point of all consciousness.

In the picture of the iceberg at the beginning of this chapter the superconscious mind would represent the entire ocean and the sky surrounding the iceberg. In fact it would even be connected to the landmass outside of the picture, the planet, the universe etc... In other words it is our connection to Source.

When you're sleeping, meditating, praying, relaxing, daydreaming or practicing guided imagery it is in this state of consciousness your enlightenment or inspired answers come from. It's also known as the Universal Consciousness. Due to human ego, many people think that this consciousness is an expansion from our consciousness that we somehow created. In fact it is just the opposite. It's consciousness that has always existed that we are a part of. We're allowed to experience it freely during our existence. In the world of pure consciousness there's no such thing as separation of being such as you and I. Everything is one and the same. If during this existence we choose to study and understand its properties we're able to communicate directly with Source, receive knowledge, inspiration, guidance and increase our lives in any way we desire.

THE GIFT OF THOUGHT

This is portion of a lecture given by Andrew Carnegies' "Science of Success Philosophy"

"Let me call your attention to a great power which is under your control. A power which is greater than poverty, greater than the lack of education, greater than all of your fears and superstitions combined. It is the power to take possession of your own mind and direct it to whatever ends you may desire.

This profound power is the gift of the Creator and it must have been considered the greatest of all of his gifts to man because it is the only thing that over which man has the complete and unchallengeable right of control and direction.

When you speak of your poverty and lack of education you are simply directing your mind power to attract these undesirable circumstances because it is true that whatever your mind feeds upon your mind attracts to you.

Now you see why it is important that you recognize that all success begins with definiteness of purpose and with a clear picture in your mind of precisely what you want from life."

Andrew Carnegie

Did you know we have approximately 60,000 thoughts a day? Think about it… Now it is 60,001. We live in a world of thought. Thought is the basis of everything and everyone. In fact even before you began reading this book some form of thought had to take place. Without having a thought of it in some form you would not be reading it. In fact without having a thought of some form you would not be doing anything. You must have thought of wanting to read and then to read this book or perhaps you had thoughts of progressing your life in some way. Maybe you've even been researching the topic in bookstores or online.

"Thought is the vehicle of creation."

Take a moment to look around you right now. Everything you see around you, before it was created in this physical world began as a thought by someone. This book that you're reading right now before it became this book was the result of many thoughts in my mind. In fact right now as I am writing it, the remainder of the book from this point forward is still uncreated. I am attracting information through the several parts of my mind from my research, past experiences and the formless substance to receive the inspiration of what is to come. Then upon imagining what I'd like to say it's then transformed into the completed reality that you're now reading. That's the process of creation. You're looking at the results of my thoughts.

If you're sitting down right now, the chair that you're sitting in began as a thought. Its creator decided he'd like to make a chair. In his mind he had the thought of creating a chair and then allowed his imagination to create. From these thoughts he designed the completed product in his mind. Even the color of the chair or whether it was painted, stained or upholstered was part of his thought process. Then utilizing this mental blueprint he may have drawn physical blueprints to work from or simply created the chair from imagination. The finished product is the chair that you're now sitting in.

THOUGHTS BECOME THINGS EXERCISE

STOP: Don't read ahead until you've completed this short exercise.

It's important that this exercise is done at the same time that you're reading these instructions. So right now take a moment to get a pencil or pen before you continue.

1. In the center of the box on the next page draw the front of a small house with a peaked roof that has two front windows and one door.

2. In each window draw four windowpanes of glass and on the door draw a small doorknob.

3. Draw a chimney on the left side of the peaked roof, with smoke coming out of it blowing towards the left.

4. In the sky you can draw three clouds.

5. In the distance behind the house draw mountains.

6. In front of the house draw a road going from left to right.

7. Now draw a walkway going from the front door of the house to the road.

8. Where the walkway meets the road draw a mailbox just to the left of the walkway.

9. On the right of the walkway in the front yard draw a tree.

10. To the left of the house draw three, stick figure people. Draw two adult stick figures and one child, which will be half the size of the adults who are waving.

11. On one of the adults head draw a tall Santa type hat and on the other draw a baseball cap.

12. In the lower right hand corner of the picture sign your name.

Draw in this box.

    This drawing you've created is an example of how thoughts become things. As you were reading the instructions your thoughts were imagining images of the instructions being given. You then created those images with your pencil or pen trying to draw as exact as possible the images you had created in your head. Once you were finished you then placed your signature on your newly created piece of art.

This masterpiece that you've created, this "thing" of beauty began with a thought. It may have been much more beautiful or different in your mind however by converting thought to reality this is your end result. This picture that you've created is proof that thoughts with *imagination* become things.

Keep in mind that this masterpiece you created isn't an original however. It's an attempted duplicate of the "thought" original but not an exact duplicate. Thoughts are multidimensional and unlimited. In their translation you drew them onto a two dimensional plane (the paper). It might have come out close to your thoughts but in no way exact. The original masterpiece remains in your mind.

A SECOND HAND WORLD

We live in a residual world of secondhand creations because the originals were created as thought. Due to the limited tools and resources we have available to us we're not always able to create things exactly as we imagine them. Therefore the original chair that we spoke of before that was in the creators mind as a thought may have been much more spectacular than the actual finished product. Through the use of his imagination it may have had rainbows emanating from it with colors that were indescribable. However due to the mortal limitations of this physical world it was made as close to his thought process as it could be.

Without the thought the chair would not have been created. As you know chairs do not create themselves. Therefore the thought does precede the action. This same concept works with everything. Every single thing that you can see which was created was initially a thought.

All communication begins with thought as well. Before you speak, you must take a moment to think about what you want to say. Even though many times it would seem that some people don't think before they speak, in actuality they did. The challenge is in verbalizing exactly what you're thinking of. Thoughts can be very difficult to transform into words.

A good example of this would be a young man desiring to tell his girlfriend how he feels about her. In his mind he's thinking of many wonderful things. His thoughts may create images filled with romantic music, fireworks and little cupids shooting their arrows through hearts. Then finally, he looks at her to verbalize his feelings and the only words that come out are; "You're cool". How would his girlfriend take those two simple words? Would she receive them in the same manner that he intended to deliver them?

In this residual or physical world of reality your words may not quite describe your true intent. They sometimes can seem to be second best, or an inferior copy of the original. Have you ever found yourself saying something to someone that didn't come out quite the way that you wanted it to? I think everyone has experienced that at least once in their life.

Even the way your body looks began with a thought. An example of this would be to look at a professional bodybuilder. The reason that they have so much muscle and are so well developed is at some point in their life they decided that this is what they wanted to be. They had the thought of being a bodybuilder. They realized through their thought process that in order to be a bodybuilder that they'd have to eat properly, exercise and be consistent in their efforts of working long hours to attain the goal that they'd desired. They didn't just go to bed one night as weaklings and wake up in the morning looking like Mr. Olympia.

The same goes for people who are energetic, overweight, healthy or sickly. Somewhere along the line a thought had preceded the actions that were taken to achieve the present results. Often times that statement raises a lot of eyebrows but even sickness was created as a thought. Many have a hard time accepting that they created their own sickness so I will explain that further.

SUGGESTION INSPIRES THOUGHT

Thoughts are created or inspired by suggestion. Suggestions are coming to you virtually all of the time, day and night. These suggestions come to you through input received from outside sources as you've learned earlier in this book. How many thoughts might go through your mind on a daily basis as a result of coming in contact with or within earshot of any of the sources of suggestion you frequent?

If you have about 60,000 thoughts each day, what are you doing with your thoughts? Are you dwelling on negativity or only the positive things you come in contact with? While you're out at the local coffee shop having morning coffee with your friends your subconscious mind is accepting suggestions. They may be coming from the TV set just a few feet from you giving the details of a tragedy that happened earlier that day? Even if you're not listening to it consciously and having a conversation with your friends, your subconscious mind is always working, recording input.

Remember the purpose of the subconscious mind is to constantly recording information. It's like a sponge accepting every bit of input within its realm of senses. Therefore everything that's going on around you that can be heard, seen (even within your peripheral vision), felt, tasted or within your sense of smell is being logged in your subconscious mind. Much of this information is what starts your thought process whether you want it to or not.

My wife and I were riding on the subway one day going into Center City Philadelphia to her hypnosis office at the 12th St Gym. As we were riding we overheard the conversation of two ladies that were sitting across the aisle from us. They were obviously acquaintances that had not seen each other in a long time. One lady said to the other, "What's your son up to these days? He must be at least a teenager by now." The other lady looking slightly agitated responded with, "You know I've been telling the little bum for years that if he didn't straighten out his act that he'd end up in jail just like his father." Then she looked her in the face and said, "He's been in jail for about six months now." We observe them both shaking their heads in disbelief as if they had no idea how this happened.

In addition to having the constant negative suggestions for most of the formative years of his life of going to jail, these negative suggestions came from an authority figure (his mother), which made them even stronger. Since birth this young man had learned to accept everything that came from his mother as factual. They became permanent programs stored in is subconscious to be referred to throughout his life. Therefore even though the boy may have not wanted to go to jail consciously you can see where he was fighting an uphill battle. His programming became a self-fulfilling prophecy of sorts. His programming led him right to jail!

RIDING BRAINWAVES TO SOURCE

In this section you will learn how your thoughts become thought waves so they can reach their destinations. As mentioned earlier, you are a thought machine.

Your thoughts don't all go to the same place. They're intended for various destinations depending on your desires. Some thoughts are intended for Conscious Mind activity such as when you are doing math or organizing your bedroom. Some thoughts are intended for Subconscious activity such as when you are dealing with pain, regulating body heat and deep breathing. Many thoughts however are intended for Superconscious activity such as when you are attracting success or failure, the perfect relationship or a nightmare date.

In the case of Superconscious or universal thought, your thoughts leave the physical constraints of your body / mind and enter the Quantum World of *universal thought energy*. This is actually done very easily ... each and every day ... by all of us.

The following brainwave states will breakdown the thought process and help you to understand what you're doing and what's been happening up until now. It will show you the profound effect that relaxation, meditation and guided imagery can have on us if harnessed for good.

TECHNICAL STUFF: Brain waves are continually generated by the electrical activity of the brain. These brain waves can be measured by the use of an (EEG) Electroencephalogram. This EEG has sensors, which are placed along the scalp of the head that monitor the activity produced by the firing of neurons within the brain. Brain waves like all other waves are measured in two ways. They are measured in cycles per second (cps.) an in Hertz (Hz). 1cps equals approximately 1hz.

NOTE: An (MEG) Magnetoencephalograph is used to measure the activity "outside" of the brain by recording the magnetic fields created by the electrical activity occurring naturally in the brain. This is done by the use of a SQUID (Superconducting Quantum Interference Device) which measures very sensitive or weak magnetic fields.

It's been found that this MEG has been able to register activity just split seconds before a thought enters the mind. This just helps to prove that our thoughts aren't limited to the physical confines of a brain or skull. Thought is not limited to a confined space and also exist outside, surrounding each person and as you'll see in the following chart even overlapping the thoughts of others. In this field or source of intelligent thought surrounding us we're able to experience intuition, insight and creative thought. We become linked mentally to so much more than ourselves. This is a source of unlimited intelligence.

A good example of how thought exist externally would be to watch a school of hundreds of fish travel in unison and in a split second all will make a course correction simultaneously without bumping into each other. There was no last-second communication between each one of them that they better change directions really fast. If that were the case, the course correction would have been made in a completely disorganized manner. The same can be seen in a flock of birds flying closely together and again making course corrections as if they were being informed by an outside source.

The following brainwave chart will show you the sequence of thought starting in High Beta. The grey shaded areas represent the expansion of consciousness as your brainwave state slows. Notice the overlapping of consciousness between the people at the bottom of the page as they enter the Alpha State. It progressively overlaps until it enters the Delta State where it becomes one consciousness.

It is important to understand that you are in all brainwave states simultaneously with one happening to be dominant at a specific time.

BRAINWAVE CHART

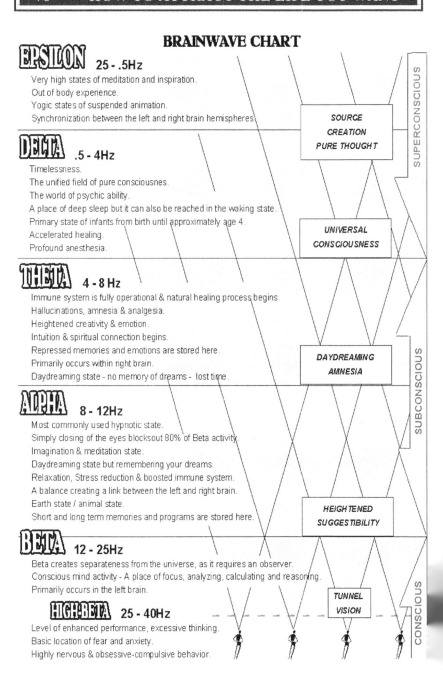

EPSILON 25 - .5Hz
Very high states of meditation and inspiration.
Out of body experience.
Yogic states of suspended animation.
Synchronization between the left and right brain hemispheres.

DELTA .5 - 4Hz
Timelessness.
The unified field of pure consciousnes.
The world of psychic ability.
A place of deep sleep but it can also be reached in the waking state.
Primary state of infants from birth until approximately age 4.
Accelerated healing.
Profound anesthesia.

THETA 4 - 8 Hz
Immune system is fully operational & natural healing process begins.
Hallucinations, amnesia & analgesia.
Heightened creativity & emotion.
Intuition & spiritual connection begins.
Repressed memories and emotions are stored here.
Primarily occurs within right brain.
Daydreaming state - no memory of dreams - lost time.

ALPHA 8 - 12Hz
Most commonly used hypnotic state.
Simply closing of the eyes blocksout 80% of Beta activity.
Imagination & meditation state.
Daydreaming state but remembering your dreams.
Relaxation, Stress reduction & boosted immune system.
A balance creating a link between the left and right brain.
Earth state / animal state.
Short and long term memories and programs are stored here.

BETA 12 - 25Hz
Beta creates separateness from the universe, as it requires an observer.
Conscious mind activity - A place of focus, analyzing, calculating and reasoning.
Primarily occurs in the left brain.

HIGH-BETA 25 - 40Hz
Level of enhanced performance, excessive thinking.
Basic location of fear and anxiety.
Highly nervous & obsessive-compulsive behavior.

SOURCE
CREATION
PURE THOUGHT

UNIVERSAL
CONSCIOUSNESS

DAYDREAMING
AMNESIA

HEIGHTENED
SUGGESTIBILITY

TUNNEL
VISION

SUPERCONSCIOUS

SUBCONSCIOUS

CONSCIOUS

HIGH BETA: 25 - 40Hz

This is a very fast brainwave state that's present is extremely busy activity. It can be unhealthy to remain in this state for a prolonged time. It can cause severe anxiety, stress and agitation which often results in fear and obsessive behaviors.

It's interesting to note however that fast brainwaves such as High Beta and higher can cause what is know as *critical mass*. This is a state where the subject can become so confused or overwhelmed due to the level of their mental activity that they become just as suggestible as they would in the very relaxed Theta and even Delta states. This confusion technique is used extensively as a way of conditioning in the areas of sports, the military and even in some business applications.

There's no spiritual application or overlapping of consciousness in High Beta. As you can see on the previous chart the expansion of consciousness is so small that it can also cause tunnel vision. You're so highly focused on your project that you can't see what's going on around you. It can also result in loss of memory for the same reason. You're shutting yourself off from your inner mind. It's similar to the effect you'd have if you were to wear the blinders that are used for horses to look ahead and not be able to see off to the sides.

Here are some of the features of High Beta:

> It's the level of enhanced performance.
> A common location of fear and anxiety.
> Excessive thinking.
> Obsessive-compulsive behavior.
> Highly nervous behavior.
> Excessive multi-talking.

BETA: 12 - 25Hz

Beta is the brain state that dominates your normal waking state when you're busy with the cognitive tasks of the outside world. It's the busy, active state of mind used while learning, working and figuring things out. It's used when focusing on the five senses of seeing, touching, hearing, smelling and tasting.

Here are some of the features of Beta:

> Everyday conscious mind activity
> A place of focus
> Analyzing
> Calculating
> Reasoning
> Alertness
> Engaged in problem solving
> When you are mentally active
> Working
> Primarily occurs in the left brain

ALPHA: 8 - 12Hz

Alpha is recommended for the treatment of stress. It's also the beginning of deep relaxation and the meditative state. It's a level of heightened suggestibility and the primary area to create positive changes in your life. It's where imagination can run free and has the ability to create reality.

Alpha is home of what's known as the Earth or animal state. In this frequency you naturally feel better, relaxed and refreshed. It's the beginning of where the subconscious becomes more dominant. Some call this feeling as being *in tune* or *environmental synchronization*.

Many Earth related religions or groups resonate with the Alpha State and conduct many of their rituals or processes there. This can be seen in the Native American, Aborigine, Wicca and many other ancient derived groups. Often times these groups will utilize, ask advice of and even worship animals, birds and Earth formations in their belief systems. Animals are thought of as bridges from this world to the next plane or what we'd understand as bridges from consciousness to the Alpha state. In fact this is true as animals reside primarily in the Alpha brainwave state and humans primarily in the Beta.

Alpha is also the state mentioned earlier where knowledge in the immediate surrounding field of birds or fish gives them the simultaneous thought information to travel so smoothly in spite of the many changes in directions.

Here are some of the features of Alpha:

Meditative state
Most common hypnotic state
Heightened use of imagination
Daydreaming state but remembering dreams
Catalepsy
Boosted immune system
Relaxation & stress reduction
A heightened state of suggestibility
A balance between the left and right brain
Earth state / animal state
Short term memories and programs are stored there
The link between the conscious and subconscious mind
Serotonin is naturally released in this state
Closing of the eyes blocks out 80% of beta activity

THETA: 4 - 8 Hz

Theta is a deeper state of relaxation that can be easily reached through daydreaming. It's the state where deeper meditation is conducted. It's also recognized by the accompaniment of amnesia. If you were daydreaming or even night dreaming and you didn't remember your dream when you awoke, you were most likely in the Theta state. Remembering your daydream would be a result of being in the deeper portion of Alpha.

In addition to experiencing amnesia it's also accompanied by the feeling of missing time. Often times upon exiting a relaxation session in the Theta state that lasted for over 45 minutes, clients will remember it to only be 5 – 10 minutes in duration. They lost the additional 30 minutes due to their crossing the line mentally into Theta.

If you notice the grey areas of the chart you'll see that the consciousness begins to overlap in the Alpha state and in the Theta state it's much more concentrated. This accounts for the increase in creativity, spirituality and intuition. You begin to feel and understand what others are experiencing at a much deeper level.

Here are some of the features of Theta:

Rapid Eye Movement (REM) sleep - deep dreaming
Natural healing process begins
Immune system is fully operational
Level of hallucinations *(seeing something that is not there)*
Analgesia: Feeling pressure but no pain
Heightened Creativity
Heightened Emotion
Intuition begins - spiritual connectedness
Repressed memories and emotions are stored here
Primarily occurs within right brain
Amnesia begins

Day or night dreaming state but not remembering them
Noticing the loss of time - timelessness

DELTA: .5 - 4Hz

This is the dominant area of deep sleep, universal consciousness and the beginning of the coma state. This is where the subconscious mind connects to and delivers messages to the superconscious mind. It's where all thoughts become things. This state can be entered through deep relaxation, sleep, meditation, hypnosis and guided imagery. Thoughts that are sent into formless substance act as a form of radar attracting anything of similar frequency.

Here are some features of Delta:

The super-conscious domain
Timelessness – Only the now exists
The still, *dreamless* deep sleep state
The unified field of pure consciousness
The world of psychic ability
The observer no longer exists as separate
Universal consciousness
Source energy
Primary state of infants from birth until approximately age two
Primary state of many elderly before death
Loss of physical / body awareness
Accessing profound anesthesia
HGH – Human Growth Hormone is released
Capable of experiencing "negative hallucinations" *(not seeing something that is there)*
Accelerated healing - a minimum of three times faster

EPSILON: .25 - .5Hz

Epsilon is a brainwave level that's not often spoken of. Here are some of the features of Epsilon:

> The coma state (Extreme healing and recuperation)
> Very high states of meditation and inspiration
> Out of body experience
> Yogic states of suspended animation

REMEMBER:

1. The nature of your conscious mind is to stay the same, to remain status quo.

2. In your quest for progress the conscious mind may try to hinder you at every turn. Be Alert!

3. The subconscious will "always" give you what you are consciously focusing on.

4. Your subconscious mind is like a 5 year old child and does not understand negative.

5. The superconscious is your connection to the Universal Consciousness or Source.

6. You have over 60,000 thoughts a day that must be monitored.

7. Everything in this world was created in the world of thought first.

8. The brainwave states will help you understand the connection between your mind and the Universe.

CHAPTER 3

THE WORLDS
WE LIVE IN

*"A chameleon can change its color to
blend into its environment but
man has the ability to change his
environment to suit him"*

Earl Nightingale

THE CHICKEN CAME FIRST *(In my reality only)*

Which came first, the chicken or the egg? Neither, either or both! Actually the thought came first. In the Quantum World not only is thought energy but also the chicken and the egg. Therefore it's all a matter of perception or preference, isn't it? If you imagined that the chicken came first, then it did. If some else imagined the egg did then they're right also. If everyone has a different reality, a different perspective of the same stimuli then who's to say who's right or wrong?

In order to describe the workings of the human mind in relation to thought it's first important to understand the concept of how we live in two different worlds simultaneously. They're the Physical World that we as solid beings are familiar with on a daily basis and the Quantum World of miniatures where everything's broken down to its smallest component.

OBSERVER AND THE OBSERVED

In the physical world we coexist with the universe as separate beings. We'll call these the Observed and the Observer. In your perspective, as you're reading this book, you are the observer. This book, everything and everyone that you can see are the observed. This is what causes the separation that we have come to know as humans. This is what gives us the sense of "I" or the sense of being an individual. Is this sense of separateness reality or is it simply an illusion? As you're looking at me you are the observer and I am the observed however in my perspective I'm the observer and you're the observed. Can they both be true or are they both illusions?

We as observers make choices on a constant basis. Even though every possibility that could ever exist does exist in the Quantum World once we, the observer come into play, the unlimited possibilities become only one possibility. The mere action of *being observed* collapses the field of possibilities to one at a time, then another and another. This is because the Observer only exists in the Physical World. The choices you make create "your" reality. With all of the people on this planet there are no two realities that are exactly the same

Here's an example of how this collapsing of the quantum field can be explained. Imagine you were driving down the road and knew there was an intersection coming up ahead of you. As you let your imagination run free you could imagine the many possibilities that can be taking place at that intersection as you arrive. You can turn left, right or go straight. You can have a flat tire in the middle of it. There could be a marching band traveling through. It could be out due to construction. You can even turn around and drive back the way you came from. There are unlimited choices in this world of possibilities and they're all happening at once. Now as you drive up to the intersection, you stop at the light and drive through it. As you're a physical being in this Physical World, you as the Observer could only observe "one" of the possibilities which was the one you chose. The process of choosing one collapsed or eliminated all of the other possibilities.

If you stopped, turned around and faced the intersection again but had your eyes closed, all of the possibilities would return again as well. Closing your eyes eliminated The Observer. Opening them creates the separation from Source and eliminates all but one possibility as before. It's the *process of observing* that creates separation from Source and collapses all possibilities but one.

The reality that you're living in right now came about as the result of your past conditioning. Whatever you've come to know as truth, whatever belief systems, preferences or understandings you have from your past is your present reality. Whatever your new conditioning or understandings are now will be your future reality. Your reality can stay the same or change drastically. It's all up to you. It's all a matter of perception. Your choices are unlimited!

THE QUANTUM WORLD

In physics, quantum is the study of all things that are small. It can be described as "the minimum unit of any physical entity involved in an interaction". It's a study of atoms, electrons, matter and as you'll find things even smaller. The quantum world can sound unimportant or confusing to those who aren't familiar with it as it's a science that most of us have never seen in school. If you take a moment to try and understand it, I guarantee you'll find it very worthwhile. Here we go...

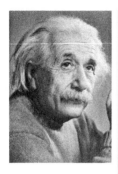

Albert Einstein: It begins was a remarkable man named Albert Einstein. Einstein, who we know today as a scientific genius of his time, spent approximately half of his life trying to find a way to unify the entire universe. He believed there was a common denominator or link to all known phenomena including matter, energy & gravity. Unfortunately in his lifetime he didn't have time to prove his theories.

Today we have scientifically proven that Einstein's "Theory of Everything" was mathematically sound. Scientist did find the source however it was not what they expected. What they found was that everything that exists within this universe from objects, living things, planets, space and anything else you can think of could be unified in a miniature world. Breaking them all down into their tiniest components they traveled beyond the Nuclear World and even beyond the Atomic World. The common denominator was in the Quantum World. In this world to their surprise, nothing was solid. It was a vibrating sea of energy. Everything that exists today, including us comes from this vibrating, living source energy. The frequency of vibration, density and arrangement of the energy would determine what it would become in the physical world. All physical things came from this non-physical, formless energy.

It's important to understand that energy cannot be created or destroyed. It's an eternal substance but it can be changed, rearranged, molded and manipulated in almost any way. Just knowing that statement alone opens a world of possibilities and questions doesn't it? This energy is actually alive, it moves, it vibrates and is consciousness. In fact it's the original source of consciousness from which we became self-aware.

One of the many things that make this Quantum World so different than the physical world is that in the Quantum World separation *does not* exist. There is no distinction between the observed or the observer. The observer being made of this same material is also part of the Unified Field. A simple way to understand would be to imagine the universe as an ocean of water and you being one drop taken out of the ocean. That one drop now has individuality very much as you do in this physical world. It contains the same building blocks, consciousness, and abilities as the source that it came from. It's self-aware Source Energy. Once that drop of water, "you", is dropped back into the ocean it now becomes part of the ocean once again rather than an individual.

Everything that exists comes from this Quantum World or this ocean of consciousness. There's nothing solid or physical in this world, it's completely made of unlimited possibilities or potential. It's "one" original, formless, universal substance that thinks, is alive and is compelled to increase, to become more than it is.

Your clothing, furniture, houses, pets, the oceans, mountains and even you, all fall within these same criteria. It has been found that even thought is made up of this energy. In fact thought is one of the highest forms or frequencies of energy. So from this discovery we realize that everything is connected, alive, vibrating and is made of the same material.

UNLIMITED SUPPLY

The Universe is also an inexhaustible source of energy or raw materials. You can never use it all up. While new thoughts are constantly creating new creations, older ones are dissolving as well. Even though the entire universe is made of it, it was not entirely used up in creating the universe. There is enough left to create thousands of universes in addition to those that have already been created.

When you're creating your goals it's important to "think big". People have a tendency to think very small in their creations. Perhaps it's because they're thinking through limitations or appearances. Maybe they feel there's not enough to go around or maybe they think if they order to big from the universe that someone else will go without. Nothing's further from the truth. The only limits are in your own imagination. There's enough to go around. It's said that in the United States alone we have enough natural resources to build a house the size of the White House for every person and still have plenty left over. No one else will go without if you think big as the universe only creates more and never takes it away from someone else to give to you. That would be against its nature and purpose. The Universe is creative and not competitive.

To the universe there's no difference between one dollar and one million dollars. Think of the universe as the ocean. You can take a glass of water from it each day for as long as you want or 5,000 gallons each day and it will keep on refilling itself. It's amazing how many people will still worry about having enough for a glass of water even with this unlimited source.

You can ask for what you need to be happy for a day or for the rest of your life. Either way you'll not drain the universe of its resources. The nature of the universe is to constantly be expanding.

If you're constantly thinking and focusing on positive things, positive things will come to you. On the same note if you're thinking and focusing on negative things, you'll be attracting negative. As you can see it's a pretty self-explanatory process that virtually anyone should understand. Understanding it and living it however can be two different things.

THOUGHT FREQUENCIES

Think of thoughts for a moment as radio waves. Radio waves and thoughts both have something in common. Neither one of them can be seen, but we know they're out there. Right now there are millions of radio waves bouncing through space all around us. Proof of that would be if you turned your radio on to your favorite station it would immediately begin playing music of whatever's on that station. The way it works is that once the music is played at the radio station it goes through a process of being transmitted outward through their radio transmitters. Anyone within their traveling radius who would care to listen to them could. Once you turn on your radio those radio waves are once again transformed through your radio receiver so they can be listened to in the form of the music that is being played on the radio station. In order to receive that specific music you must tune your radio into the exact radio frequency that the radio station is transmitting on. Therefore if the radio station is transmitting on 97.5 your radio must also be set to 97.5 to receive it. Your radio being set at 97.5 will attract and receive any frequencies being transmitted on 97.5.

Thought works the same way. If you're thinking positive thoughts of getting ahead in business for instance, your thoughts are being sent out or transmitted in every direction similar to a radio wave. Rather than being sent out into the air however, they're being sent out into the

Universal Consciousness; the formless void of Source Energy where everything exists as one. Remember this strong thought power is a higher form of energy or vibration. Anything that's of a similar frequency to that thought of success in business such as positive opportunities, people or circumstances will be attracted back to you. On the other hand if you're thinking of how rotten a day you're having, those frequencies are also being sent out and will attract many additional negative things that will help you to continue having an even worse day.

QUESTION: If you were listening to a radio station that you didn't like would you continue listening to it or would you tune into another station?

Of course you'd change that station as soon as possible so you could listen to something you enjoy.

In the same manner if you're not happy with your life the way it is now then you must change your present way of thinking to attract something you enjoy.

What frequency are your thoughts tuned into right now? Are they tuned into:

97.5 "The Sounds of Success" station or are they tuned into 85.3 "The All Night Depression" favorites?

Keep in mind that when you're having negative thoughts you have the ability to change your frequency just as you have the ability to change the station.

How many people do you know that listen to the all day and all night victim stations? Here are some of the ones I'm speaking of:

The I just can't get ahead no matter how I try station.
The no one likes me station.
The I hate my job station.
The I always feel sick station.
The bad relationship station.
The 24-hour woe is me station.
The I can't pay my bills station.

You may have listened to some of those in the past as well but how easy would it be to change the station to:

The everything I touch turns to gold station.
The everyone loves me station.
The I love my job station.
The I feel healthy, happy and terrific station.
The I have great relationships station.
The 24-hour why I like me station.
The I have enough money for anything I want station.

It would be great if there were some kind of child monitoring device that we could put on our thoughts to block out negative thoughts and only allow the entertaining or positive thoughts. Unfortunately you're the only monitoring device you have. The choice is yours. You must decide which station you want to listen to. They're all available and there's no competition for one or the other. Whichever you choose, you get.

OPPOSING FREQUENCIES NEVER ATTRACT

Here's a fact that Science and Religion agree upon. Good thoughts can "only" attract good thoughts. Good cannot attract bad.

Here's the scientific explanation: Thoughts as you know are frequencies which are similar to radio waves. In both cases you cannot see them, smell them, touch them or taste them but they're still there. Thousands of wave frequencies right now are hurdling through the air from televisions, computers, cell phones, radios and even thoughts just to name a few. Similar to radio frequencies, a frequency of 97.5 will only attract 97.5. Even though many other frequency waves are there they cannot be attracted unless you're on the same frequency.

Here's the religious explanation: "Make a tree good and its fruit will be good, or make a tree bad and its fruit will be bad, for a tree is recognized by its fruit. Matt 12:33. For a good tree bringeth not forth corrupt fruit; neither doth a corrupt tree bring forth good fruit. For every tree is known by its own fruit. For of thorns men do not gather figs, nor of a bramble bush gather they grapes. A good man out of the good treasure of his heart bringeth forth that which is good; and an evil man out of the evil treasure of his heart bringeth forth that which is evil; for of the abundance of the heart his mouth speaketh. Luke 6:43

This is like saying that nothing can come from corn but corn, nothing from nettles but nettles. Men understand this rule when it comes to nature but have difficulty when it comes to them. Positive thoughts of health and wealth cannot and will not bring anything negative. In order for negative to come, it must be invited.

IMAGINATION – THE 6TH SENSE

> *"Imagination is the fuel for thought.*
> *It gets the mental vehicle moving."*

You have learned that thought is the beginning factor of everything. If thought is the *vehicle* then you can look at imagination as the *fuel* it takes to get it moving. One without the other is useless. Once a thought comes forth the imagination takes over so as to create what to do with it. Therefore everything is determined by imagination.

As you've been reading this book you may have been imagining how you can utilize it in your life. You may have been imagining how you can use its teachings to help your friends, family or clients. Once you receive the thought to begin this process your imagination becomes active with creativity showing you countless ways that you can use it.

Keep in mind the difference between imagination and visualization. When using visualization you're able to see things that you've actually seen, experienced or understand from your life. Imagination covers that and so much more. Utilizing your imagination has no restrictions or boundaries. Imagination doesn't involve sight, sound or any of the other five senses.

THOUGHTS: Consider imagination your 6th sense.

It's the key to creating both the physical and quantum world. It's the basis of suggestibility and all self-help.

If you can imagine something then it's possible.

If you can't imagine something you won't be able to attain it either.

You can imagine real people transforming into cartoon characters. You can imagine them flying and turning into birds. You can probably even imagine that I were taking a bright yellow lemon and cutting it in half right in front of you … then taking one of the halves and squeezing it very slowly so that the juice begins to drip down all over the table. Upon using your imagination you would not only be able to imagine what that picture would look like but you may even have found your mouth watering as well.

SUPERCHARGING WITH EMOTIONS

"If thought is the vehicle for change and imagination is the fuel to move the vehicle, then emotion supercharges the fuel."

Emotion is the key to *quickening* the imagination process. Emotions put out extremely powerful vibrations into the universe. If you're trying to attract something into your life such as health, wealth, improved relationships or happiness, applying positive emotion in the process will greatly enhance it.

There are literally hundreds of emotions that humans are able to experience. Of the hundreds of emotions approximately a dozen are experienced on a regular basis. Then out of those emotions approximately four of them are positive. This helps to show why so many people find it easier to be negative than positive.

Think about when emotions are shown. When bad things happen such as losing money, becoming sick, a death in the family, losing a job, getting in a car accident, becoming hurt, being insulted or belittled, being passed by for a promotion or when not being appreciated, we often times display very negative emotions. These emotions can range from anger, sadness, rage, disappointment and disgust. When positive things happen however such as receiving money, getting a promotion, getting your car fixed for free, being complemented or appreciated, all of the positive emotions associated with these are not nearly as intense as the previous negative ones were.

THE ULTIMATE GIFT

Imagination is a wonderful gift that we've been given as humans. One of the greatest benefits of utilizing imagination is the ability to use it to create *permanent change*.

*"The subconscious mind doesn't understand the difference
between an imagined or a real memory.
They each hold the same value."*

Once you understand and more importantly accept that statement,
you'll truly see the power of imagination begin to change your life.

CREATING REALITY WITH IMAGINATION

Imagination is used to create your reality as well as to create a new
one. Take a moment and think about reality. Is everyone's reality the
same or do they have the ability to create their own reality? You'll find
that reality does change from person to person. No two people share
the same reality.

A good example of this concept is to imagine yourself and a friend
having both gone to the same restaurant together. As a result of the
meal you found the food and the service to be wonderful. In fact you
thought it was the best food you had ever eaten. Your friend however
did not enjoy his food and found the staff to be quite rude. Later on
that evening your friend developed food poisoning and became
violently ill. Once your friend had a chance to recuperate you and he
got together again and discussed your experiences of the restaurant that
you had eaten at. Your realities of the same restaurant after just a short
time will be quite different. You'll look at the restaurant as a
wonderful place to eat and will probably want to return soon. Your
friend on the other hand would look at the restaurant from this point
forward as a terrible eating establishment that should be shut down. He
would have a very negative outlook on the restaurant and would
probably tell as many people that he comes in contact with to avoid
going there. Notice how both you and your friend ate at the same
location however your realities of the experience are totally different.

What are other topics where people's realities are completely different due to their upbringing, memories learned propaganda and experiences? Here's a list of just a few. As you read through the following list take a moment to examine how you feel about each choice. There'll most likely be one that will resonate with you more than the other. There may be one that you like and one that you extremely dislike. That's your reality. However the point of this is to understand that everyone doesn't share your same reality.

> Harvard or Yale
> Cadillac or Mercedes
> United States or United Kingdom
> Health food or junk food
> Pepsi or Coca-Cola
> Renting or owning
> Buddhism or Christianity
> Coffee or tea

Now that you've read the list you probably have strong feelings towards certain ones. These feelings or decisions that you've made to choose one over the other had been developed through past conditioning of learned propaganda and repetition throughout your life You may even think of a preference you had years ago that's completely different today. Many times you'll hear people say that the're not the same person that they used to be.

Here is a story about twin brothers that will help you understand how people's realities can differ depending on their situation or what you will come to know as "self image":

There were twin brothers who were raised in the same household however once they were grown and on their own they led entirely different lifestyles. Upon interviewing the first brother he spoke of how he had a great life and was very happy. He was married to a wonderful woman, had two intelligent children and lived in a very nic home in a quiet neighborhood. He had a job that he loved and was quite successful in business.

He said that he owed his success to his upbringing. His mother raised him up as his dad walked out on them when he was only eight years old. His mother later turned to drugs and alcohol as a way to deal with her depression. Because of the drugs she was unemployed and they lived in a rundown tenement building in a very bad part of the city. She was often quite abusive and he and his brother would spend most of their time at friends or on the street until they were old enough to leave and start a life of their own. It was because of this past that he was successful. He made a decision that he didn't want that life for his family. He was determined to learn from it and appreciate everything that he had.

Then the second brother was interviewed. He spoke of how he was very unhappy and had a miserable life. He had tried to get married but due to being a drug addict she left him after only one year. He had not been able to get a job anywhere and was often in trouble with the law. Presently he was living on the streets and spending most of his time scrounging food and trying to find a place to sleep. He then went on to say that the reason for this was because of his upbringing. He spoke of how his father walked out on him when he was only eight years old and how his mother turned to drugs and alcohol as a way to deal with her depression. She could not get a job and was very abusive to him and his brother. He tried to spend as much time away from home as possible by staying at friends and on the street. Eventually he had lost all his friends and had been living on the streets since. It was because of this that he could just not get ahead.

Both brothers went through the exact same experiences but created entirely different realities. One created a wonderful reality by taking control of his life and refusing to be a victim. The other made a choice to remain a victim of his situation and had a very unhappy life.

You're the creator of your own reality. You're the Michael Angelo of your life. You have the opportunity to accept it as it is and let it continue going in the same direction or to change it completely. You have all the tools that you need at your disposal within you right now. Just imagine how your life could be, and now, create it.

MEMORIES CAN CHANGE

THOUGHTS: There's not a separate compartment in your mind that's unaffected where your memories are stored. Your memories are stored in the same place as your feelings, desires, imagination and everything else. Your memories aren't absolute, constant or the same. When your reality changes, in many cases your memories will change to accommodate them.

A good example of this would be if you were ever at a family function where two or three siblings were speaking about things that happened to them when they were younger, often times you'll hear each one of them recalling their memories slightly different. One might remember the event as being very happy while another might say it was the worst thing that ever happened to them. Their recollections may differ in what happened, the location where it happened and even their ages when it happened. In many cases some people even deny that it ever happened at all.

Here's another interesting concept that you may be familiar with. I know of a woman who was such a chronic liar that eventually she began to believe her own lies. She was so unhappy with her life that she created a sort of fantasy type past of being a victim that actually helped her to rationalize her present life. Through repetition she would continue saying the same things happened over and over, which is the same process of how faith is developed. You'll see later in this book how this process of utilizing your imagination with repetition and belie will actually re-route your neural connections so new ones can be formed thereby making the false memory a real one. This is also the same process used in creating new habits.

> *"If you do anything long enough it will eventually become a habit and part of your new reality".*

By understanding how this process works you'll be able to use your imagination along with the process of repetition to replace, change, or create virtually any belief or memory you'd like.

FALSE TESTIMONY BELIEVED TRUE

The positive side of being able to change memories is that if you have negative memories that are haunting or hindering you from progressing right now, they can be replaced.

The negative side of this is that most of the public are not aware of how memories can be changed and become permanently engrained in as little as a few weeks. Once the new memory becomes engrained, even if it's opposite of the actual truth, it will become a belief. You would even be able to pass a lie detector test to attest to the truth of this new memory.

Just imagine how many innocent people may have been sent to jail in response to sworn testimony or a *lie detector test* results that were thought to be true but in actuality, completely false. The memory of the witnessed event or crime within the first couple days may be true, but what if it was fuzzy or unclear? The witness trying to make sense of what was happening can and most likely will develop a completed memory by filling in the blanks with their imagination of what happened. That can happen automatically just to have peace of mind or to make better sense of it when talking about it.

These blank pieces or changes can be created or fabricated by suggestion from other witnesses, prejudices, fears, lawyers or many other stimuli. The witness will swear to them as truth because it will be true in their newly developed memory. The bottom line is not to place too much stock on the memories of the past as it's over, behind you. Focus on the now and on creating new memories.

"Do not go where the path may lead,
go instead where there is no path and leave a trail."
Ralph Waldo Emerson

REMEMBER:

1. In the Physical World there's separation of the observer and the observed.

2. Unlimited possibilities exist in the Quantum World. It's a world of thought, energy and connected to us through the superconscious mind.

3. Thoughts in this substance can only attract thought of similar frequencies.

4. Imagination is the creative force that makes things become reality.

5. In the Quantum World there's no separation. It's a unified field of oneness.

6. Memories are not absolute; they're changed as our lives change.

CHAPTER 4

HINDRANCES
TO SUCCESS

*"One of the main weaknesses of mankind
is the average man's familiarity with the word
impossible.
He knows all the rules which will not work.
He knows all the things which cannot be done."*

Napoleon Hill

PLAYING THE GAME EXERCISE

STOP reading this book right now and do this exercise before you go any further. It will really help you understand more about yourself!

Answer these questions honestly. Write your *immediate* response to the questions. Your *first impulse*s before you have a chance to rethink them. Those are your true thoughts.

To get the best effect, complete one question at a time and don't read ahead until you've answered your present question.

Questionnaire

Are you happy with your life?

_____

What could possibly make you happier?

_____

_____

_____

Why has that not happened yet?

_____

_____

_____

_____

Do you want to be rich?

_____

If you're not rich already, what stands in your way?

_____

_____

_____

Do you want to be healthy?

_____

If you're not healthy already, what stands in your way?

_____

_____

_____

Do you want a great relationship?

_____

If you don't have great relationships already, what stands in your way?

_____

_____

_____

Now look at all your answers and see if any of them include blame, justification or complaining. If they do then you are playing the victim game. You now have something to start improving. If not, you're on the right track. In order to be truly successful at anything in your life you must take 100% responsibility for your own actions.

THE VICTIM GAME

No one's "naturally" a victim. No one's born a victim. They must become a victim. Being a victim is a choice just as not being a victim is a choice. It's a game that people play to rationalize their behavior, give them attention and excuse them from being successful or to find the easy way out.

Here's one of the most important lessons that you can ever learn.

> *"In order to be truly successful in any undertaking*
> *you must take 100% responsibility for yourself.*
> *Victims cannot be truly successful."*

One of the major things that stand in people's way of progress or attaining their goals is the lack of taking responsibility for their own lives. This is also known as "using the victim excuse".

The victim game comes into play when you feel that you need to place blame, justify or complain about why things are the way they are in your life. Do you know of anyone who plays this game? Someone who's heard to say; "Poor me. Why do things like this always happen to me? It's not my fault, or I just can't help it."

When you're playing the "Poor me" routine you're attracting to yourself exactly what you place your thoughts, focus and attention on. You in turn will draw more of that negativity to you.

Playing the role of the victim alleviates the stress of failure. It's an excuse to not have to take responsibility or to achieve. Victims are people pleasers. They want to be noticed and crave attention. Victims are primarily and almost entirely concerned about themselves; the "It's all about me" attitude.

Here are the three main characteristics of being a victim.

1. Blame - People who usually play the victim game are very good at placing the blame on others for their problems or failures. They're professionals at finding someone to point the finger at.

You're either a victim or the target of a victim. Victims are notorious at blaming their spouse, family, parents, religion, society, employer, government, customers, God, the devil and even their tennis racquets for their shortcomings.

2. Justify - They tend to say things like: "Money's not that important to me." If money weren't important to them then they wouldn't be seeking after it constantly. You'll also find that those that say money is not important to them are most likely broke. It's a justification of their not having enough money for their needs.

Another one is, "I don't really need friends anyway." This is a classic for those who can't get friends for whatever reason. It's a justification of what they can't acquire. Remember the basic rule of the subconscious mind; whatever you focus your attention on you attract to you.

Complaining - Most people who complain all the time tend to have think they have tough lives. After all, what are they attracting to them but more of what they're complaining about?

Some people love to complain and seek out the companionship of others who love to complain as well. They sit and listen to each other just waiting for their turn to complain about what's bad in their lives. Negative energy is very contagious!

Years ago I was a U.S. Army drill sergeant. When approached by a trainee with an excuse of why he couldn't do a certain task I would respond with, "Excuses are like elbows, everyone has one." You see, it doesn't really matter what the excuse is if you don't want to do something. One excuse is as good as another. In other words if you asked me to borrow five dollars my response could either be, "no, I really can't loan you five dollars right now because things have been slow at work." Or I could say, "No because the stars aren't in alignment with Jupiter right now." If I don't want to loan you the money, then the excuse really doesn't matter. The answer should simply be "no". The excuse has no bearing on the question. You either want to loan the money or you don't, it's that simple. Going back to the military, the trainees were taught to answer any question with one of three statements and they were, "Yes, No, or No Excuse." That's the difference between being a victim and taking 100% responsibility.

One of the main reasons people play the victim game is to get attention. Victims confuse attention with love. Victims show love for what others can "do for them", not for who they are. They feel the need to "buy" love or attention rather than deserving it or being worthy of it.

> *"Long term repetition of behavior is known as identity.*
> *Feeling stuck with the behavior is called an addiction.*
> *Complaining about it is called validation.*
> *The opposite of this is known as responsibility."*

Using these excuses repeatedly will create a *habit* of being a victim. You're now getting into the realm of what is called "career victims". Take a moment to think about the people that you know. I'm sure you can make a list of these folks. Maybe you're even guilty of this behavior. If so keep in mind that since it's a created behavior, it can b changed. As a way of shedding more light on this phenomena, take a moment to answer these questions:

Do you know anyone who when asked to do something challenging will say that they can't do it because it's something they've never done before?

Do you know anyone who is afraid of making a decision?

Do you know anyone who seems to complain about everything?

Do you know anyone who prefers to rationalize another's success in a negative way rather than congratulate or be proud of them?

Do you know anyone who feels they can't get ahead in life due to their nationality, background, sexual preference, their past, the neighborhood they live in, their spouse, their children, their parents, their job, their present finances or lack of, their health, their relationships, their loneliness, their depression, their government, their education level, their busy schedule, their lack of familiarity, fear, or even lack of sleep?

THOUGHTS: After reading the previous questions you are probably now beginning to see the scope of how large this "playing the victim game" really is. It's so huge that it could probably sustain itself as a major religion. On the other hand there would probably be too many excuses for it not to get started.

Being a victim is a choice. You're not born with it. If you weren't born with it then you must have created it.

Being happy or angry is a choice.

Deciding to act positive with a smile on your face or negative with an attitude when you meet someone is a choice. Being happy of course will probably help you to achieve your goals and even receive assistance from those who you're dealing with. Being negative will most likely be responded with negativity and create an uphill battle with pretty much anything you're trying to attain. Remember the old saying that you attract more bees with honey than vinegar. Especially when you're not feeling well or having a bad day, you still have a choice of displaying your feelings of negativity or a choice of putting a smile on your face. Which would you rather be on the receiving end of? You attract what you put out.

Have you ever heard anyone say that when they get angry they just can't stop? Is there a *gene* within the human being known as the *anger gene* that keeps them angry for six hours, twelve hours or even two days? Of course there isn't, it's a choice to remain angry. It's also a choice that as soon as you realize you're angry to stop immediately. Have you ever known of anyone who was in the middle of an argument or being angry that felt they could not stop but when the phone rang they immediately answered it with a very cheery voice as if nothing had ever happened? That was also a choice.

Being wealthy or poor is a choice.

If being wealthy is your goal then you must approach it by taking 100% responsibility for your actions and go for it. That's a choice that you must consciously make without wavering. It's also a choice for you to give up, complain about how hard it is or to rationalize with one of a hundred of excuses why you can't accomplish it. The result of which one you'll receive, success or failure is your choice.

Having more bills than income is a choice.

It's funny how adults with their developed sense of responsibility seem to act more like children than children do when they see something that they want. There are more toys available for adults than you can imagine such as jewelry, perfume, cosmetics, power tools, recreational vehicles and the list goes on and on. Adults see something that they want and if they can't afford it they finance it. Then all of a sudden in addition to their normal monthly expenses that must be paid, new bills begin arriving for credit cards, fancy cell phones, vehicle payments, power tools and so forth.

If you went back however to the point before they actually purchased or finance these items. No one was holding a gun to their head. They weren't under the influence of an armed assailant forcing them to buy that new car that they could not afford when there was a used one right beside it that fell within their budget. No one forced them to buy that diamond ring or to go to the Mall on a shopping spree to buy new clothes with their credit card because they were feeling down. Those were all choices that they consciously made.

Getting a better job or keeping one that you hate is a choice.

Time and time again in my capacity as a coach I see people who feel that they're stuck in a rut with their present job. However because they're used to it rather than trying to find a better job that would make them happier, they simply continue their present one and complain about how everything is so bad. Even though change can be inconvenient and in many cases frightening it's still a choice to remain in an unhappy situation rather than to do something about it. The purpose of life is to be happy. If you're not happy with your life because of your job, career, relationships, location or whatever it might be, you have a choice to do something about it.

Feeling sick or great in the morning is a choice.

QUESTION: When someone comes up to you and asks, "How do you feel today?" How do you answer them?

Do you immediately respond with something positive such as, "Wonderful, great, spectacular, awesome or better than I've ever felt?" Or do you actually take a few seconds to contemplate on your aches, pains or maybe even scratchy throat and tell them exactly how bad you're feeling? You have a choice of doing either one however remember that wherever you're placing your thoughts, focus and attention that's what you're drawing more of. So if you're feeling sick or under the weather and someone ask you how you're feeling, unless it's your doctor or medical professional, tell them that you "feel great".

There have been many times in the morning where I woke up with a scratchy throat, a fever, a headache or just not feeling well in general, but rather than complaining and sharing this negativity with everyone I would act as if I felt wonderful. When someone asked me how I felt, I would say that I felt great. Why? It's very simple; by placing my thoughts, focus and attention on feeling great and even expressing it with emotion I'm drawing more of these great, healing feelings to me. Then inevitably what would happen is within a very short time I'd actually feel just as I was saying; great.

Deciding between exercising or eating sweets is a choice.

You have a choice to be healthy or not. No one's forcing you to eat sweets, cake, or anything else unhealthy. That's a decision for you to make on your own. As for exercise, although it may be uncomfortable to get started since it is something different than you may have done before, keep in mind that if you do it anyway it will eventually become a habit and thereby easier to do. If you do it with a positive attitude with a smile on your face it will become even easier.

RESISTANCE TO CHANGE

Another hindrance to progress, which you read in an earlier chapter, is the conscious minds approach to change. The conscious mind's a creature of habit. It doesn't like to change or to be inconvenienced in any way and will cling to its old ways as much as it can even if it knows that this behavior is hindering progress. The conscious mind will always fight to remain the same, to stay within its comfort zone, and enjoys what's known as the *status quo*.

Being aware of this trait of the conscious mind is a very important factor to your progress. Whenever you feel resistance towards change, laziness in the face of progress or start rationalizing that maybe the way your present way of doing things is "okay after all" rather than trying something new, realize that this is the habitual response of your conscious mind fighting change. Unless you become aware of this trait and actively combat it you'll remain stagnant in your progress.

"There's no same. Life's in a constant state of transition."

Progress, attaining goals, becoming wealthy, healthy or having better relationships require change. It requires inconvenience, doing something different, letting go of the same and more to the point it requires really "shaking up" your life. The more you stretch or the more that you can go outside of your comfort zone the closer you are to attain your goals.

If you are *comfortable* in your life then chances are that you are not progressing. If everything seems easy, you are getting nowhere.

Comfort is synonymous with digression. In other words you're either moving forward or backwards. There's no same. Everything in life changes, it's always in a state of transition. Even all the cells in your body within a relatively short time will be completely renewed. So this security that the conscious mind has in thinking that it's remaining the same is actually a false security. You're either progressing or digressing; there is no other choice.

LIMITING BELIEF SYSTEM

Many of the limiting beliefs that you have about your capabilities stem from the memories and experiences of your past. You may have been told or experienced many things, especially from those who are close to you, giving you suggestions such as:

You're not good enough to do that.
Don't try that, there's no way you can win.
That only works for rich people, it never happens to me.
You should be happy with what you have.
Don't try that you'll get hurt.

Those negative statements have become ingrained in your mind and throughout your life may have acted as a mental handicap toward your progress. You can break free of your past conditioning and remove the restraints. The only limitations that you have are the ones that you place on yourself.

Have you ever gone to a circus and noticed how a very small chain is restraining the large elephants? In some cases instead of a chain on a rope is tethering them. With the strength that an adult elephant has, how is it that he can't break free from his restraint? The answer to that is that he was conditioned. He believes that he can't break free. When circus elephants are young, very strong heavy-duty chains are used to restrain them. Of course the young elephants having as much energy a they do will try and try to break free of these restraints but won't be able to. Eventually they'll stop trying, realizing that it's futile. This creates a limiting belief system in them. Later on when they're fully-grown and could break the chain with very little effort they won't even try due to their conditioned belief that they're created.

We're the very same way as humans. When we've been repeatedly told that something's a certain way, we may challenge it however will eventually accept it as a belief and usually not test it again. Such was the case of the four-minute mile. For years it had been said that no human could break the four-minute mile barrier for running. It has been attempted many times and was taken for granted that it was just impossible. Then in 1954 Roger Bannister, a 25 year old medical student from Harrow broke the four minute mile by running it in 3:59:4. If that's wasn't extraordinary enough, within 46 days his rival John Landy broke it at 3:57:9. Over the next three months 16 more runners did it. Now that the mental conditioning or block was gone from this rule, you can see the four-minute mile being broken quite often even in high school and college track competitions.

You must let go of past limitations and learn to utilize and appreciate your greatest asset, which is your mind. What the mind can conceive it can achieve. If you can imagine it then there's a way that you can do it. Look at all the great achievements that have been attained by man. When you look at the many marvels of mankind realize that those who have attained these achievements, those unbelievable results, are people just like you. You have the same capabilities, resources and opportunities as they do. The bottom line is if they can do it so can you.

How do you break out of this mental conditioning? One way is to believe in yourself and don't accept what you're told. One of the greatest abilities that you have as a human is the ability to think outside the box. You have the capability to examine yourself as an outside observer. You have the capability to change, grow, and exceed your own expectations. Set your specific goals, believe in your ability to attain them and don't deviate from your path of going for it. You have the ability to "Reach for the Gold".

How do you challenge yourself? How do you know that you're doing enough to progress? One of the best ways is by referring to your feelings. How do you feel about your goal? Is it a comfortable feeling? If so then you are probably not extending yourself enough. In creating a challenge for yourself you should make it a bit scary. You should always think big in your decision making process and if the thought of attaining your goal in addition to being a bit scary creates excitement, then go for it. Now you have a challenge.

I'm not saying that your life should be a gamble. Of course before you jump into anything you should have your eyes open and research it first. You would never jump into a pool of water without checking how deep it was before hand. What I'm saying is, get out of your comfort zone and strive for more than you think you can do. Reach for your potential. Remember the slogan;

"If you do the same things for the next five years as you did the last five years, five years from now you will be in the same place that you are today."

Unless that's what you want, stretch yourself and do something different now.

LACK OF PERSEVERANCE

An extremely important step in the process of attaining your goals is perseverance. Lack of perseverance is one of the main reasons why people fail. It's similar to the gestation process of a plant. You can't simply plant a tomato seed and expect to eat tomatoes immediately. There's a time of gestation that must take place. In this time of gestation the seed germinates, sprouts, grows and eventually bears fruit. During this time it must be watered, fertilized and weeded. The time between planting the seed and picking the fruit is considered the gestation period.

Imagine going into a restaurant and when the waiter arrives you order a bowl of soup. The waiter goes into the kitchen to place your order, which is being prepared. When the waiter comes back to your table you decide to change your mind and tell him that you would now like a salad instead. Now the waiter returns to the kitchen to turn in your new order for a salad, which is being prepared. As the waiter walks by your table you stop him and tell him that you changed your mind and you would like a sandwich now. The waiter returns to the kitchen to place the order for your sandwich. At this point you've been waiting quite a while since you changed your order several times and you're becoming dissatisfied that you've been waiting so long. Being frustrated you get up and leave the restaurant without receiving your food.

The important thing to realize is that you did place your order, which was turned into the kitchen and started each time. Due to your impatience you didn't wait for any of them to be prepared *(the period of gestation)* as you continued changing your order and finally left the restaurant. However in the kitchen there's a bowl of soup, a salad and a sandwich that were made for you. So even though you were too impatient to wait for your food, it was prepared and there in the kitchen waiting and is possibly going to be enjoyed by someone else. You made a conscious choice to give up.

NEVER GIVE UP: How long must you continue working toward your goal? Until you get it! If it's something that you truly want then you must never give up. If you're persistent and you believe that you will get it, then you will.

It's amazing how when you're able to see your goal most people will continue working towards it until they receive it. If you bought tickets to go on vacation to Disney World with your family for instance. Once you began driving to Disney nothing would stop you until you arrived. Even in the face of obstructions, detours, distractions or delays you would continue going to your goal because you know it's there. This is the same frame of mind you should have towards attaining any goal. Remember the universe has already created it and it's waiting for you. So keep the image in your mind that it's there and persevere until you reach it.

FEAR - *False Evidence Appearing Real*

In our lives fear of the unknown can add great stress to a situation. Walking into a dark room, being late for work or even receiving an unexpected past due bill that may be larger than you can presently handle. Fear seems to take on a life of its own as it spirals out of control.

This section will teach you exactly what fear is, where it resides and how to eliminate it. It's important to identify fear as soon as it arises and eliminate it for many reasons. One of the most important reasons is that it's a major cause of stress. Stress immediately shuts down your immune system leaving you open to sickness, depression and multiple other disorders which you will learn in an upcoming chapter.

Some of the most common causes of fear that are totally unnecessary are listed here as a way to help you to identify and eliminate them. They are fear of:

The Government	Death	Taxes
Terrorism	Gods Wrath	Failure
Success	Persecution	Bill Due Dates
Retirement	Public Speaking	Flying

The Dark   Taking Exams   Your Future
The Playground Bully

NO FEAR IN THE PRESENT

If you find this type of behavior happening to you, stop yourself for a moment and ask, "How am I doing at this very moment?" You'll find that at this very moment that the certain financial obligation isn't affecting you whatsoever. In most cases you'll find that at this very moment you have food, shelter, and warmth. This very moment you have all that you need and you're fine. It's the fear of the unknown that causes the anxiety. To look at it another way, it's the "Boogieman" hiding in the closet or right around the corner. The actual fear that you had is something that's not happening now. Each new day brings with it new challenges and opportunities. It's like opening a Christmas present. You never know what is inside, what surprises lie right around the corner. So whatever your challenges may be, keep in mind the present. You're okay right now.

There's no fear in the present. Fear only exists in the past or in the future. When you're afraid of something you're afraid of what may happen or what had happened. What's happening right now is okay and if you can focus on the present everything else associated with it will be okay as well.

FEAR CAN STALK YOU

Many times your imagination will create situations of fear, stress and anxiety simply because it was not controlled. This is just another reason why it is important to control your thought process. An example would be the experience of Mary who was at a late-night party her friend's house, which was in a bad area of town. It was almost 11 M when Mary realized that she had not finished working on a project that she needed to have completed early in the morning. She decided to leave the party early to go home so she could finish.

Upon leaving the party Mary had to walk down several dimly lit alleyways to get to where her car was parked. As she got approximately one block away she imagined that she heard footsteps behind her. Becoming anxious she began to walk faster. As she was walking faster she was sure that she was being followed by someone as she could hear the footsteps matching her own. She began running as fast as she could to her car. She was very afraid that whoever was following her had their mind set on robbing her. Now, fearing for her life she finally reached her car, got inside and sped off as quickly as she could.

When she got home Mary called her friend to let her know what happened, warning her to be careful that someone was lurking in her neighborhood. Mary's friend began laughing as she told her what was going on. She told Mary that everyone who walks down those alleys late at night says the same thing. What's actually happened is that the sound of Mary's shoes while walking in the quiet created an echo through the alleyway, which made it sound like someone else was walking behind her.

This is why when Mary sped up her walking; the sounds of the footsteps matched her speed exactly. Mary's fear was a result of an over active imagination. However sometimes an over active imagination can be the thing that saves you.

THE GHOST OF FEAR

You can think of fear as a ghost or something that doesn't exist. A example would be not having enough money to pay your electric bill. You may be afraid that the utility will be shut off. Then the fear begin to spiral that if the utilities are shut off you won't be able to cook; the there's the heat for your house, your computer and so on. You begin to worry that someone may call you, harassing you to pay the money. It's almost as if you imagine someone like the Boogeyman standing in the middle of the street outside of your home waiting for you to leave so he can grab you. You've created this imaginary fear that doesn't exist standing in the street outside of your home. So this fear exists in the future.

Right now however, in the present everything's fine. Right now you have electricity. Right now you have lights, heat, and your computer is running. If you're living in the moment there's no reason to fear. Much can happen before any action would be taken to shut off your electricity. Maybe you'll receive some unexpected money in the mail. Maybe you'll get a paycheck from work before it comes due. Maybe the electric company will even give you a month extension. In other words there's nothing to fear if you allow things to simply be as they are.

There's a saying that you may have heard that states, *"The only thing to fear is fear itself."* If you live in the present there's nothing to be fearful of. Everything right now is fine. At this moment, you're reading this book, probably sitting or standing and if you're immersed in the book chances are that you're not thinking of what's going to happen in the future because your mind is focused on my words. You have no fear right now. Congratulations by the way.

The only thing that you should have to fear is fear. Why, because fear causes a whole range of difficulties beginning with stress, anxiety and even depression. However fear does not have to give you any heartache at all if you don't give it power. Remember fear is simply a ghost. It's a figment of your imagination that's not really there. It will not bother you, or harm you in any way.

FEAR IS NOT REAL

About eight years ago I was teaching a clinical hypnotherapy certification course in Biddeford, Maine. One of my students was a Psychiatrist named Jim from Pennsylvania. We had just finished conducting a practice hypnotherapy session on a volunteer who came to the school with her family. During the break I overheard Jim speaking to the teenage daughter of the client that we had just finished with. In the conversation she had mentioned to him that she would very shortly be leaving home for the first time in her life with an organization called "Up with People".

This was an organization that was going to take her to various countries throughout the world where she would be a performer of sorts with a large group. She mentioned to him that although she was very excited about the trip she was also very scared. Her fear was due to the unknown as well as being on her own for the first time. In part of this conversation I remember Jim asking her, "Where is the fear? Show it to me. I want to see it." To this she replied, "I can't show it to you. It's in my head." There was then a short pause between the two of them and looking at her face I noticed what I can only describe as an "Aha moment". She got it!

The fear that had been crippling her all this time, getting in the way of her enjoying the excitement of this upcoming experience was something that no one else experienced except for her. It was a choice that she had made and like any choice could be changed. It was like shadows lurking in the dark. All she had to do is turn on the lights and they'd be gone.

HOW TO ELIMINATE FEAR OR PAIN

Here are two ways to eliminate fear. The first one is simply by using the principle of acceptance. The second is to change the properties of fear from being subjective to objective. In fact, these principles in addition to eliminating fear can also be used to eliminate anxiety and even pain.

> **WARNING:** If you do use these techniques as a way to eliminating pain, please check with a physician in advance. Remember pain's a warning sign that something's not right with the body and should be paid attention to. Do not attempt to relieve pain unless it's been reviewed and approved by a professional medical practitioner.

1. Acceptance - The opposite of acceptance is denial or pushing away. This is exactly what most people do when they experience fear. Rather than accepting it they try to push it away, to run from it. Whenever you push something away you tend to increase it. Remember whatever you're fighting against, you'll get more of.

Instead, take a few moments to examine the fear, attempting to label it as much as you can. What are you afraid of? Why are you afraid of it? How does that make you feel? Why? What options do you have? How would this situation be any different without the fear etc.? By accepting the fear and identifying it you're bringing it into a manageable range. It's important to realize that life is as it is; that whatever you're feeling right at this moment is the very best that life has to offer you right now and it's okay. Within this remarkable life we get to experience happiness and joy; however, they would not be appreciated nearly as much unless we had the opportunity to experience sadness and even fear. Realizing it just for what it is and allowing it to be, will lessen it and in most cases eliminate the fear altogether.

2. Make it objective - Fear is subjective. You can't see it or show it to anyone. It's in your head. Therefore, by making it objective you're literally changing it to something else, to a physical object. If it's a physical object then it has changed and cannot be a subjective fear anymore. You have changed its very nature and it no longer exists. Just as when a caterpillar turns into a butterfly. Once the transformation has taken place it's no longer a caterpillar. It has transformed and is now something entirely different, a butterfly.

ELIMINATING FEAR OR STRESS: *(exercise)*

NOTE: The key element in this exercise is to use your imagination. It can be done anywhere at any time. It does not even require closing your eyes if you don't want to. However closing your eyes may make it easier to use your imagination.

*(***WARNING:*** *This exercise works equally as well for pain but it's imperative that before you use it on yourself or anyone else that you or they have been checked out by a doctor. Remember pain's a warning signal that there's something wrong with the body and must be attended to by a professional medical practitioner.)*

*****Here's how it works*** *... This is what you'd say to someone or think to yourself if using for self-help purposes. Keep in mind that I do this with clients who come to see me or over the telephone so I'll be reciting it here as if I'm saying it to a client.*

"I'll be asking you questions and I'd like you to answer me out loud.

Now, close your eyes and focus on the fear you're now experiencing. (Closing eyes is not required but helps to enhance senses)

Imagine that you're able to place the fear (or pain) inside of a box ... how large of a box would you need? (Wait for an answer)

If the fear had a taste ... what would it taste like? (Wait for an answer)

If the fear had a sound ... what would it sound like? (Wait for an answer)

If the fear had color ... what color do you imagine it would be? (Wait)

If the fear had a smell ... what would it smell like? (Wait for an answer)

If you were to hold this box in your hands ... how heavy do you think it would be? (Wait for an answer)

Now, imagine all of these together. Imagine the fear inside the size box you chose ... imagine the taste ... the sound of it ... the color ... the smell ... and the weight. Get it all clear in your mind and imagine as if you're holding it in front of you right now ... Nod your head when you have accomplished that.

Now open your eyes. The fear is gone."

f the fear or pain has not completely left your client by this time, which it usually does, then have them do it over again if needed to iminate the remaining fear. Try it, it works great.)

OUR PAST MAKES MOST DECISIONS

Do you realize that approximately 90% of all the decisions you ake on a daily basis are determined by your past? If you didn't, don't el alone. It's not a bit of trivia that's taught in school. It's interesting at only 10% of a specific task is decided by the task itself. Three ople may approach the exact same situation and react quite differently. One might be excited over it, the second may feel indifferent towards it and the third may be scared to death over the situation.

When faced with making a decision

90% - Comes from the past
10% - Comes from the present

Take a moment to go back to the beginning of your life when you had no experiences, likes or dislikes as of yet. From that point forward you began to accumulate experiences otherwise known as memories. If you touched something that was hot you got burnt. If while running you fell down and got hurt this was another undesirable experience.

Let's imagine for a moment that when you were six years old you were riding your bicycle with one of your friends through the woods. Suddenly you approached a small stream that had a long plank stretched across it. You watched your friend as he easily drove right across the plank so you decided to do it also. As you drove across you went too far to one side as both you and your bicycle went crashing down to the stream. As a result you received a sprained ankle as well as many bruises and scratches. Now years later as an adult you find yourself walking through the local park hand in hand with your girlfriend. As you're walking down a path through the woods you approach a stream that needs to be crossed. Stretching across the stream is a large fallen tree that is quite wide and seems to be well traveled. Your girlfriend tells you to follow her as she runs across it quite easily. Now it's your turn; you look at her and say, "I can't do it, I'll find another way around."

Basically what happened is; seeing the tree going across the stream triggered an emotion in your subconscious mind linking you back to when you first felt this emotion. That's when you were a six-year-old and fell off the plank with your bicycle. Immediately, anxiety and fear arose creating doubt of your ability to pass. Therefore your decision was made primarily from the past rather than from the actual challenge itself. Even though you're now an adult, on foot and it's a very large tree your response is still very cut and dry. You won't do it.

YOUR PRESENT LIFE BLUEPRINT

How many decisions do you make on a daily bases that are determined by your past? Do any of these decisions that were decided upon from your previous experiences hinder your current progress? All of your experiences of the past have created a blueprint or map of the person that you are now. The limitations that you've developed when you were younger still remain.

QUESTION: Where did these limitations come from?

Remember, you were not born with limitations. You were born perfect, free of any negativity. Limitations were taught to you by those who raised you or influenced your growth is some way. In many cases the habits, morals, ideals and restrictions that your guardians had would also be part of your blueprint. Whatever you had observed, heard or experienced from those who raised you became part of your blueprint. Their actions were the only reference that you had towards approaching various situations.

When you begin to examine why you act a certain way or have specific reactions to any given stimuli take a moment to reflect on what you had observed, heard or experienced about this specific stimuli from your parents. If for instance you seem to have a self-sabotaging reaction to saving money, think back to what you observed about how your parents saving money. Did they spend it as soon as they received it? Did they often discuss how they had such a difficult time saving money? If so do you find that you have the same problem? Chances are good that you might.

When you're working towards attaining a goal ask yourself what your parents' opinion of what you're doing would be. Would they think that this type of a goal was silly, attainable, a waste of time, wise or only something that the more fortunate people do? If so these restrictions that have become part of your blueprint will have to be changed in order for you to be successful. It's a form of conditioning that must be addressed. What's standing in your way of success?

"What you've seen, heard or experienced from those who raised you often became your life blueprint."

All of these memories and experiences of your past have developed you into the person that you are today. They've determined your self-image or who you feel yourself to be. They've determined your reality; your perception of life. They've given you the handicaps or the exceptional skills that you have to succeed. The question to ask yourself is has your past given you the habits to excel in attaining your goals or has it given you unlimited hurdles that must be overcome?

THE GOOD NEWS

The good news is that these habits of the past that made you who you are today can be changed. Just as you have developed the positive or negative habits that you presently have, a similar process can be used to get you back on track or to propel you even quicker to your destination.

This process will be discussed in detail later on in this book. All of your past memories, lessons and experiences made you who you are today. All of these things have determined your present self-image.

How you react to things in the present came from your past. Your past experiences are what you presently use as a gauge to make decisions.

Even a Supreme Court Judge must rely on his past experiences, education and memories in ordered to determine the guilt or innocence of an accused. The judge listens to the arguments of what had supposedly occurred but makes his judgment based on his past conditioning. Now what if that conditioning was wrong? What if the judge were to practice law in an entirely different country with different rules? Then the judge would have to completely recondition his training to reflect the new rules. He'd have to completely replace his old habits of decision-making with the new, proper and pertinent habits of the new location he's practicing in. If he didn't do this he'd be continually making wrong decisions as 90% of his decision-making process comes from his past experiences and he'd most likely be thrown off the bench.

We all have the same problem. Think about it for a moment. As a child you were brought up by your guardians according to their standards of health, wealth and relationships, which were probably taught to them by their guardians and environment. Throughout your upbringing you developed the blueprint that you'll use for the rest of your life in the way of how your health "should" be, how financially secure you'll be and what kind a relationships you'll have.

Look back at your guardians right now. Would you be happy having the same kind of health, wealth and relationships that they did? If you'd like more out of life than they had then you'll have to change your blueprint to something different just as the judge did in order to progress with his job in a new location. Are you willing to break your family traditions of being the same in order to progress?

AWARENESS OF LIMITATION

As you go throughout your day from this point forward keep what you've just read here in the front of your mind so you can consciously choose to make decisions on the current and proper information at hand rather than from your past. When you're preparing to make a major decision take a moment to think back to how your parents would have reacted to this decision. What would they have said or done? Would the decision they would have made be the same that you would? If your answer's yes then that decision seems to be the proper one for you. However if your decision is the same that you remember your parents making and as a result of that decision you see hardship, hindrance or limitations then be aware of this thinking process. Now you have the opportunity to consciously create a new decision of proper thinking.

Awareness is the first step in making proper choices. Imagine for a moment what it looks like being in the driver's seat of an automobile. Notice how in front of you there is a large windshield to see where you're going. As you look up towards the top of the windshield there's a tiny rearview mirror. The tiny mirror gives you a view of what's going on behind you as you're driving. Use this analogy as your model for life. As you're traveling through life realize that what's ahead of you is so much more important than what is behind. Keep your eyes to the front and focused on the Gold.

REMEMBER:

1. Being a Victim is a "game" that people play.

2. There's no such thing as a born victim.

3. Victims **complain**, **blame** and **justify** rather than take responsibility.

4. Being a victim is popular and contagious. It justifies their unsuccessful behavior.

5. Fear's not real and can be reduced or eliminated.

6. You're presently the result of your past experiences.

7. What you do now will determine who you'll be in the future.

8. Be aware of limitations to growth so you can attain your goals.

CHAPTER 5

THOUGHT
TRANSPLANT

*'The only thing about a man that is a mans' is his mind.
Everything else you can find in a pig or a horse."*

Archibald McLeash

WHAT IS A THOUGHT TRANSPLANT

A thought transplant is a non-surgical procedure in which your old way of *appearance* or *environmental thinking* is replaced with a new way of *elite thinking*. It's a way of thinking only what you *want* to think. In life we each create our own reality.

"You are the Creator"

By being the Creator of your own reality only you are responsible for what you allow into it. If you wish only positive thoughts of health, wealth and happiness such as what you were promised at birth that's what you'll receive. It's thinking that anything contrary to these promises does not exist. Negative does not exist. This new way of thinking must be exercised and built-up similar to any muscle if it's to be developed successfully.

This is a radically different way of thinking than most are used to. It may be difficult to grasp in your present situation since you have never practiced it. As you begin your transformation you'll gradually begin to see your reality change. You'll become a different person than you are now. Upon continued practice the concept of thinking according to truth and what you want will become easier and be adopted as your new lifestyle.

NO ONE HAS EVER TAUGHT YOU

No one had ever taught you the "proper way" to think, so you think as you were taught or observed from those who raised you. You can see this entire process described completely in Chapter 1. You were raised according to the group or how everyone else in your environment was raised. You were conditioned to think according to observations rather than what you want. In fact you didn't believe that you were destined to be, have or achieve anything you wanted. Through observation of the group you were taught exactly the opposite. You were taught to think according to limitations and restrictions. You were taught that truly great things only came to special types of people. You were taught that you were destined to achieve what everyone else around you achieved and to be happy with it.

RIGHT THOUGHT

Our thoughts create our perceptions of reality. No two people's reality is exactly the same. Each is based upon the individuals' perception of what is occurring. It's based upon their viewpoint, the angle that they're observing from and even the outside stimuli surrounding them.

I heard a story about 3 people who took part in an experiment and were asked to describe what they were about to feel in front of them. They were blindfolded and led into a room where they were placed standing around an elephant. One of them reached forward and was able to feel the tail to which he described it as a strong rope. One reached out and felt a leg to which he thought it was the trunk of a tree and the last one feeling the side of the elephant thought it was a big piece of leather. Then the blindfolds were taken off to surprisingly see an elephant standing before them. It's as if everyone has a different filter on the lenses that they use to experience life. Because of this we can never see things as they really are.

No matter how thoroughly one person may explain a concept to another the concept will never be accepted in the exact same manner that it was meant to be. This can help you to understand how concepts such as a stellar phenomenon, political speeches or even a simple verse from the Bible can be described or translated so many different ways.

THOUGHTS: We only see our version of how things appear through associations with our embedded programs which become our perceptions. With this understanding even science with its formulas and proof that identify everything within our world cannot be understood as an exact science as it's based on perception.

The influence of a group or society on the creation of our thought can be overwhelming. Outside opinions have such a strong bearing on our perceptions. For a moment imagine that you were an employee of a large firm. You're being paid a decent hourly rate for doing your job. Upon arriving at your office you notice that there's a note on your desk from your employer. It states that you're receiving a promotion and will be given a large salary that greatly exceeds your present hourly rate. The note says that the boss would like to interview you for this promotion at one o'clock this afternoon. Your immediate response upon reading the note is one of excitement and gratefulness. You're excited about all the great things you'll be able to do with the additional income and you're grateful that your boss has finally noticed the great work you've been doing.

As the time of the interview approaches you meet one of your coworkers and tell him your wonderful news. Your coworker then begins to tell you how he feels this is the boss's way of taking advantage of you. Because you'll be on a salary he can have you work twice as much and in the long run you'll be getting paid even less. He told you that this is the boss's way of saving money by not having to hire another employee.

Compare the different thinking process of how you feel now after hearing your coworker opinion to how you felt earlier after reading the note on your desk. Can you see the effect of outside thinking or thinking according to appearances? What other people say has such a great impact on those who aren't able to or willing to control their thinking. You went from being excited to being upset before you even had your meeting with the boss. You reacted to appearances.

THE DANGER OF APPEARANCE THINKING

A few years back I met a gentleman who worked as an administrator in a Virginia hospital. He told me of an instance that took place where he worked where several employees decided to conduct an experiment on a coworker who we'll name John... John came into work as he usually did on this specific morning acting and feeling much the same as he usually does. As he was going about his business one of his coworkers came up to him and said, "John you don't look too well today, is everything alright?" John responded by saying he felt fine and continued with his business. A few moments later he ran across another employee who looked at him and said "John, do you have a cold or something, you look sick." John looked a bit confused but replied that he was fine again and continued with his work. After about 5 minutes had passed a third employee approached John once again mentioning how he was not looking very well and asked if he was okay. Within a relatively short time John was seen looking at himself in the restroom mirror for a while after which he went to the boss and asked to be dismissed for the day because he wasn't feeling well.

Did the suggestions from the group actually make John sick? Was it actually John's thinking process as a result of the observations everyone was making about him? If John was able to think *through* appearances would have realized that sickness is a choice and would have remained healthy. *Thinking through appearances* is a process of original thinking. It's utilizing Elite Thought.

"What luck for rulers that men do not think."
Adolph Hitler

Just take a moment to think of the impact of this quote. Throughout all of recorded time men have been taking advantage of people in tremendous numbers for the purpose of so many atrocities such as in the case of Hitler.

People have a tendency to follow the group, and of course since the group is made of many other individuals their mentality is to also follow groups. It becomes a world of follow the follower. Everything seems to be gauged around the group so that each person thinks as the group thinks relinquishing their right to think independently. After all it's much easier to be told what to think than to think in opposition of the group. Groups need to be led. They require someone to follow and once they find someone whom they think is qualified they'll quite often follow them blindly. The group mentality becomes hypnotic and through *peer pressure* can be coerced to do almost anything.

Throughout history there've been a *select few* who understood the process of how to utilize this *elite thought* process. This process was once secretly protected and taught only to select leaders or people of importance. By keeping this process away from the masses, leaders were able to control their followers easier. As a result of this, large organizations, religions and radical groups sprang up where these followers were continually used as ponds at the whim of their leaders. Millions were killed in wars, crusades and genocides.

Some of these groups of followers and religion began to grow so large that many military and political leaders such as the great Constantine found ways to use them for their political gain. As a result there has been more murders and killing in the name of religion than any other purpose. The blind obedience or following of the group is very similar to the process of sheep or cattle being led off to slaughter.

Although in the past only a select few understood the secrets of this elite way of thinking and it was purposely kept away from the general public as a way to maintain power over them; today it's available to everyone. Anyone who'd like to break away from the group to improve their life is able to. You can find the process right here in these pages.

You'll now learn the reason why even though the secret of thinking in this elite way is available to all that most will still remain in their group or mindless cycles.

EFFORT IS REQUIRED

> *"Thinking is hard work, that's why so few people do it."*
> Albert Einstein

Every man has the natural power to think what he wants to think. It requires far more effort to do so however than it does to think the thoughts which are suggested by appearances or the group. To think according to appearance is easy; to think only what you want in spite of appearances is difficult. It takes much more strength than you'd imagine.

If you look at the appearance of disease and sickness around you, you'll produce thoughts of disease and sickness in your own mind. This in turn will surely attract it to your life as well. You must continually think of only what you want; that sickness is only an appearance and that it does not exist. You must think that there is only health. That's your birthright; that is how you came into this world before all the conditioning and limitations were programmed into you and anything else is a disorder.

If you look at the appearances of poverty, it will produce like thoughts of poverty in your mind. Focusing on these thoughts will attract poverty to your life as well. You must continually think independently and realize that it's only the appearance of lack and that there's no poverty. You must think that there's only wealth. That's your birthright and anything else once again is a disorder.

THE MASTER MIND

> *"More gold has been mined from the thoughts of man*
> *than has ever been taken from the earth."*
> Napoleon Hill

To think of only health when in the midst of disease or to think of only wealth when in the midst of poverty takes strength and practice. Anyone who can attain this ability has attained the ability to be a master creator. You're the creator of your Reality. You're the only one that can allow creation in your reality. Whether you choose to create poverty or wealth is your choice and no one else's.

> **THOUGHTS:** To do what you want to do you'll have to learn the ability to think the way you want to think. It's extremely important to remember that every thought you have is a creation in the quantum world of thought. That formless substance of thought energy is waiting to be molded with your commands which are your thoughts. Every one of your thoughts is being created whether it's of perfect health, wealth or happiness. However every thought of appearances through your environment or group, of sickness or poverty are also being created.

Once you truly understand this you're able to create whatever you want to create. You'll lose all doubt, limitations or fear. This is "the secret" behind all creation. This is what the *select few* since ancient times have always known and have kept away from the masses for thousands of years. This is what's available to you right now if you're willing to put forth the effort.

"You do become what you think about most of the time."

WHAT DO CELLS TELL US

According to modern biogenetics we are told that perception controls your behavior, your health and your genes. Therefore we can control our health or sickness at a cellular level according to our belief and perceptions of our reality using our imagination.

Tests have been done with human cells in the laboratory by placing individual healthy cells in various environments to see their reactions. In each case it was found that a healthy cell would gravitate towards other healthy cells to be healthy and to continue growth. When placed by unhealthy cells it would travel in the opposite direction as a means of safety or protection. Their choices were either growth or safety. They could only choose one because they could not do both at the same time.

Once the cells are taken out of the laboratory and become part of your body rather than reacting to their environment under the microscope they would now react to the perception of your environment. By adjusting your perception you could control their behavior.

We as humans are made up of over 50 trillion individual cells. Everyone one of these cells has this same embedded program of the ability to choose between growth or protection. Now as this ecosystem of many cells, our body still responds to signals in the same way as the individual cells did.

SCIENTIFIC BRAIN JARGON

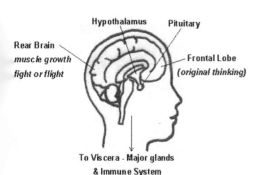

Rear Brain
muscle growth
fight or flight

Hypothalamus   Pituitary

Frontal Lobe
(original thinking)

To Viscera - Major glands
& Immune System

Here's the scientific version of what happens to you. The hypothalamus is the part of the brain that is the initial receptor or gauges the perceived signals. When you become stressed it activates your pituitary gland, which is the tiny master gland that controls your body.

The pituitary immediately constricts the muscles related to stopping the blood flow to the viscera, which is the area of all your major glands and your immune system. The blood constriction also shuts down the frontal lobe of the brain, which is required for original thinking. In doing this the additional blood flow is directed to the rear-brain which is responsible for muscle growth, quick reaction time, bone growth and strength. It's also the part of the brain responsible for the "fight or flight".

When stressed you do become stronger and have a quicker reaction time but you have also shut off other parts of the body required for nutrition, health and intelligence. You have basically resorted back to your primitive self. This is ideal if your stress is due to a car about to run over you or if you need to protect yourself. In these cases you'll have the added strength and agility to run or fight. If it's stress due to having to take a test however, you'll be less intelligent, most likely not remember most of your answers but you'll feel a strong urge to run away and hide somewhere in the corner.

YOUR IMMUNE SYSTEM

In hospitals when patients are given organ transplants or skin grafts, doctors will usually give them stress hormones to shut off the immune system so the foreign body introduced into the system won't be fought off. Without the stress hormones the immune system of the patient would naturally fight off the new gland and reject it.

On the other hand think of what happens when a patient with a life threatening illness is told by their doctor that they only have two weeks left to live. If the patient becomes stressed or as in the case with most patients, extremely stressed due to their impending death their immune system will totally shut down and often times the patient will die on the exact date that the doctor mentioned. For those that understand the power of suggestion, we also call that type of statement given by the doctor a "death sentence". A suggestion coming from someone in authority is always stronger and usually acted upon. This negative result from a suggestion or belief is also called a Nocebo.

THE DEATH SENTENCE

Let's take a moment to examine the patients that were given this type of death sentence but reacted in the opposite manner. Occasionally when given this devastating news a patient will say something like, *"If I only have two weeks left to live then I'm going to go on vacation, spend all of my money and have a grand time."* By letting go of the daily stress and having a Grand Time they've opened the blood flow to the immune system, viscera and the frontal lobe. The healing process now can begin and often times when the patient returns to the doctor in two weeks for their checkup the terminal illness had mysteriously disappeared.

The patients' perception of life, their reality for those two weeks was one of happiness, love and healing. Disease or negativity cannot reside in a happy, healthy body. This person began thinking according to personal desire rather than appearances. There's no sickness, only health. Now you're beginning to see the value of this process of thinking through appearances" or thinking only what you want.

THOUGHTS: Of all the growth promoting signals that are available to us as human beings the most powerful one is love. Love's even more powerful in the area of growth than nutrition, but do not neglect nutrition as it's also very important. When parents offer their children love, the children will grow healthier and happier. When we offer even animals or plants love in fact it's been proven that they will grow better.

Traits to enhance Growth: *(health & intelligence)*

Love	Relaxation	Laughter
Exercise	Having Fun	Happiness
Meditation	Hypnosis	Prayer
Yoga	Uplifting Music	Being of Service

Traits that signal Protection: *(fight or flight)*

Fear	Anger	Anxiety
Stress	Greed	Fighting
War	Judgmental	Worry
Depression	Overwhelmed	Confusion

THE DEVISTATING EFFECTS OF STRESS

So here is what we've learned about the devastating effects of stress When Stressed:

1. Your *viscera shuts down* as your veins are constricted and blood is sent to the rear-brain. Your viscera are all of your major vital glands.

2. Your *immune system shuts down*. You're now open to sickness, disease and weakness.

3. Blood to your *frontal lobe* has also been diverted to the rear-brain, so it *shuts down* as well. The frontal lobe is your highe thinking center. It's where your original and creative thought that aren't programmed come from. When you're not using your frontal lobe you're in fact less intelligent than normal.

4. While all this is happening, all the additional influx of blood has been rerouted to your rear brain. The part of the brain

that's responsible for *fight or flight*. It's all being put towards strong muscles and bones, speed and quick reflexes.

This action happening in the body would have been great in primitive times when man was constantly in danger of being killed by wild animals or similar dangers. When confronted by a lion the extra blood being funneled to the rear brain would give primitive man extra fuel for speed to run or strength to fight. Higher thinking, the immune system or healthy viscera wasn't as important at that specific time as survival. Once he was out of danger and relaxed the blood would be rerouted back to the frontal lobe, glands and immune system so he could recuperate from his ordeals and plan a better strategy when confronted by the lion again. The point is that he was only in the stress situation for a short while and the problem was quickly solved so his recuperating bodily functions could return.

Today stress is so much more prevalent in our society. In primitive times man only had to worry about himself and his family. He had no idea what was going on in the world and neither did he care. He was living in his own little kingdom. The difference is that we now have television, radio, internet, the news, magazines and many other forms of communication all telling you how bad the world is. There are wars, major disasters, corruption, forest fires, murders, thefts and the list goes on. Turn on the television and the majority of programs are geared negatively such as reality shows, detective and talk shows exploiting every form of deviate behavior imaginable, soap operas, police drive along videos etc. Stress abounds in virtually every aspect of life.

People get so programmed with their routines of going to work, then home, bills, television and back to work that they don't take time to relax. With all of this stress in the course of a day it's practically impossible for the immune system to have a chance to work properly. It's constantly shut off. Since the higher brain isn't having a chance to work people keep their robot type of thinking and continue with their routines unaware of what's going on. This is why sickness is so prevalent in our society.

Imagine this scenario for a moment: Imagine a small productive city in the Midwest that's very active in industry and farming. Everything's working like a well-oiled machine. Suddenly the air-raid sirens are sounded as there's a threat of a huge tornado heading through the city. Of course with the sirens sounding everyone would seek shelter in bunkers and pre-made shelters. The shelters have been created for people to survive safely and are stocked with enough food, supplies and water for about 3 weeks. Once everyone from the city's in the shelters the entire productive city would come to a screeching stop. No more production, commerce or farming would be going on for the time being. After the storm passes by the "all clear" siren would be sounded and everyone could leave the bunkers and return to work or home again. The city would be moving forward as before.

What would happen if the "all clear" was never sounded? What if everyone was in the bunkers in this state of ready but never came out? Soon the city would begin to fall apart. Crops in the fields would spoil. Production would be non-existent, utilities would fail and utter chaos would bring the city to a shambles.

That's what is happening to people today. They live in such a stress society that they begin to live in an "on-guard" state, but the "all clear" has never really sounded. The city or their health isn't kept up with and the immune system cannot do its job. Eventually sickness, depression and disease occur.

NEUTRAL IS'T GOOD ENOUGH

You must realize that neutral or just stopping stress is not good enough to get the machine running again. Look at the following colors

GREEN - YELLOW - RED

GREEN is the growth state - YELLOW is the non-stress state and - RED is the stress state. You can see from this example that NOT being in stress is still not the GREEN or the growth state. It's a neutral state or limbo. The growth state is an *action* state. It requires just as much action to move ahead as it does to digress. Lack of action or doing nothing isn't growth or movement. It's simply lack of action. So to get your immune system, viscera and frontal lobe moving, it requires action. See the previous list of traits to enhance growth and you'll have many examples of what you can do.

THE FRONTAL LOBE

The *Frontal Lobe* is a *non-ordinary* state of thought that can change your reality. It's similar to the Great and Magical Wizard of Oz hiding behind the curtain. It's such a small portion of the brain and it has the ability to change everything. Once relaxation techniques have begun and the blood flow has returned to the *Frontal Lobe* you're now in *state of creativity*. While in the use of the frontal lobe you're in a *timeless state of creating reality*. This is *the only place* where positive new change can take place.

That was such an important paragraph that I'll now break it down. The reason that the frontal lobe is a non-ordinary state is that it's the ordinary state of man to be run according to the subconsciously stored programs of the past. Without the use of the frontal lobe your life's almost entirely being operated by these programs. This is the robotic life I spoke of earlier. Many people are so caught up in the stresses and routines of live that they may go through their entire adult live without ever utilizing this place of original thought.

QUESTION: Is it possible to go through life without using this part of the brain?

Quite easily, if you think about it. Animals don't have the use of a frontal lobe and they live their lives quite well.

If you have the intent of learning the information in this book to begin using your frontal lobe then you can consider yourself in the top 10% of society.

In their natural state people are constantly running programs from their past and going about their routines just as their environment is. In order for there to be positive change as we mentioned, there needs to be a change. That can only occur with the frontal lobes creative thinking. There can be no change in "same".

When you're in the process of using your frontal lobe whether it's in meditation, guided imagery or even hypnosis you'll realize that time seems to stand still. You'll be unaware of what's going on as normal outside of you. This is the place of creativity. This creativity that brings about change is what shapes your reality to something different than it is now. So when you're in this state of using your frontal lobe you are "the Creator". You're directly sharing in the creative powers of Source.

SLOW DOWN TO MOVE AHEAD

This is exactly opposite of what we're taught growing up. We're taught to work hard for our income. The harder you work the more you'll benefit. That's actually not true by the way. We've been seriously misled with this nugget of programming. Have you ever heard the slogan "Work smarter, not harder"? By taking the time to relax each day to go into meditation or guided imagery you're able to better plan your life and to keep it on track.

According to statistics, 90% of society doesn't have any goals. If you don't know where you're going then how are you going to get here? By taking the time to relax each day and use your frontal lobe you can plan your life. You can find a direction and begin to work towards what you want to do in life rather than what you have to do. You're in the driver's seat controlling your reality rather than just letting it happen. You'll find that the more you slow down to quiet your mind the more successful you'll be.

REMEMBER:

1. Replace appearance thinking with elite thinking.

2. There is no sickness, poverty or discouragement in elite thinking. They're all disorders created by improper thinking.

3. You must slow down to move ahead.

4. Prolonged stress will make you sick and less intelligent.

5. Relaxation allows everything to work at peak performance.

CHAPTER 6

GOALS TO ORDER

"Man is a goal seeking animal.
His life only has meaning if he is reaching out
and striving for his goals."

Aristotle

CREATING GOALS

> *"Goals do not care who have them."*
>
> *Zig Ziglar*

Zig Ziglar was one of the world's greatest sales trainers and motivational speakers. In one of his presentations he spoke of a three day long test that had been conducted sometime back with college students. It had to do with their reactions to being deprived of dreaming. In this experiment he told of how the students were outfitted with electrodes attached to their heads that were connected to a machine that was able to measure their brain activity and identify exactly when they began dreaming.

Throughout the first evening of the test as the students went to sleep they were monitored closely by these machines. As soon as it appeared that the students had begun dreaming they were disturbed so as not to be allowed to do so. The second day upon waking up it was found that the students' attitudes were quite different. They appeared to be agitated and very restless.

The second night the test continued and each time they began to dream once again they were disturbed so they wouldn't. In the morning when the students woke up the results were more severe. The students were showing extreme signs of fatigue, anger and stress.

The test was continued one more evening in which the same process occurred. On the third morning as the students woke their demeanor was much worse and it was obvious that they were heading down the road to severe mental problems. The test was then terminated before any harm could occur.

As a result of the test it was obvious as Mr. Ziglar had stated in his presentation that, "When you're sleeping you need to have your dreams." Then he stated that in a similar manner, "When you're awake you also need to have your dreams."

These *dreams* he was speaking of are your goals. He then went on to say that a person with clear defined goals *cannot be depressed.* By having clearly defined goals a person knows what direction they're working towards. They look forward to waking up in the morning and working on their goals. They're positive and excited for the future.

CONTROL YOUR DESTINY

The direction of your life is determined by the decisions you make or that are made for you in reference to the constant input that you receive. Each moment of the day you're receiving input and suggestions by either seeing, hearing, feeling, sensing, tasting or smelling. The human mind is like a sponge constantly taking in everything within its influence. Throughout your day you're receiving thoughts and facing challenges or decisions that must be made. Some are very simple such as should you take a right or left turn and others are more complex such as should you invest in a certain stock or not.

By simply doing nothing you're still faced with choices. How long should you do nothing? Should you do it here or there? Should you check your messages? If you don't make decisions on the input or suggestions that you're continually faced with they will be made for you by default? If you're not making a decision to buy the last fresh loaf of bread on the bakery counter someone else buying it will make that decision for you. If you hesitate on deciding to take the parking space in front of the post office within a few seconds someone else will. In other words life goes on and will continue to do so whether you make decisions or not.

> *"A man without a goal is like*
> *a ship without a rudder."*

Imagine a sailboat for a moment in the middle of a large lake. As you may know a sailboat is powered by harnessing the wind in its sail, which propels it forward. In addition to harnessing the wind it also utilizes a rudder. The rudder is the part of the steering mechanism that is in the water connected to the sailboat designed to steer or guide it so it can go in a straight line. Without the use of a rudder the sailboat cannot be controlled or directed by its captain. Instead it's at the mercy of the winds and will most likely be blown all over the lake with no specific direction in mind.

> *"If you fail to plan, you plan to fail"*
> *W. Clement Stone*

This plight of the sailboat is very similar to your life. If you don't make decisions or have goals as to where you want to go, the direction of your life will be similar to the sailboat that's being blown about aimlessly by the winds. Your goals, the decisions that you make are your rudder in life. If you want to get somewhere you must know where it is you want to go and plan how to get there. Once you've created your plan, the rest is a simple task of just following it.

WISHFUL THINKING

Many people want to get ahead and many even have "dreams" of what their ideal life would be like. Hopes or dreams cannot be cashed at the bank, will not put food on the table and in the end, unless clearly defined and acted upon are no more than "wishful thinking".

It's funny what came to mind when I was writing this paragraph. Most of my life I've often thought about how wonderful it would be to win the lottery. I sometimes imagined what I would do with my winnings. It's a very enjoyable thing to daydream about. Then suddenly it hit me that in my entire life I had never bought a lottery ticket.

"Thinkers think and doers do."

I was speaking to one of my past graduates last week asking him how his progress was coming with starting a new business that he had been planning to open. His response was rather interesting. He told me that he had been thinking about it just about every day. He mentioned that he had lots of good ideas that he had been planning on for a long time that were sure to bring in a lot of cash.

The difference between thinkers and doers is that thinkers think and doers do. They act. All of the good ideas in the world will not pay for your bills. Have you ever tried to pay for your telephone bill with an idea?

Unless you have gone through the process of writing down your goal and created a clear detailed plan on how you're going to attain it, it's not a goal. It's still simply a wish or a dream. A well-defined goal can be attained. A dream will always be elusive and just out of your reach. Until it's acted upon it's simply an illusion.

WHY HAVE GOALS

If you'd like to progress or change your present situation in life you must have a plan. A goal would be considered a detailed plan. It's your plan of action. It's the step-by-step process or map guiding you to your destination.

Most people go through life with hopes and wishes of progressing and having better situations than they have presently. You can hear them talking about it all the time. They say that they hate their job and want something better but do nothing about it. They say that someday their ship will come in but have no idea exactly what ship that is. They state that they're open to change and willing to try anything new however they continue doing the exact same thing day after day. But simply having a wish or desire is like going somewhere with no specific destination. There are many nice places to go but without having a specific destination you'll simply drive around in circles.

> *"**Success** in uncomfortable, pushing yourself, taking immediate action, stretching and reaching for the stars. **Failure** is remaining comfortable, playing it safe, taking no action, status quo and reaching for the remote."*

Change requires action. It requires that you do something different that you've done. If what you've been doing has not gotten you where you want to be by now then it just makes sense that you must do something different. It's amazing how many people will continue doing the same thing and expect different results.

What does it take to create new goals? What will it take for you to leave your comfort zone? It will take hunger. You must be hungry for what you want; you must have a strong driving desire to attain your goal. If it's simply a whim, chances are you won't exert the energy to attain it. It's interesting to note how the majority of people who have risen to great wealth seem to have one trait in common. Many of them had begun as the result of living a life of poverty, destitution, tragedy, extreme sorrow or hitting rock bottom. It's as if they could sink no lower and had nowhere else to go but up. They were hungry not only to become wealthy but especially to get out of the situations they were in and to ensure they never went there again.

QUESTION: So is hunger the key? Does anyone who wishes to be wealthy need to lose everything and become totally destitute before it happens?

Of course not, but by realizing this similarity among wealthy people you can learn exactly what it takes to become successful in any undertaking. It takes 100% commitment. It takes an all-consuming desire or hunger to get ahead. It takes a type of commitment where you'll not accept failure in any form.

They all had a driving force that kept them moving ahead without the option of looking back or having a safety net. Unlike those who are mostly living in their comfort zone, they had nothing to fall back on. That's the kind of dedication that you need to have to attain your goals.

"Are you hungry or are you comfortable?"

I heard a story of a group of warriors who were at war fighting for their lands against an enemy that outnumbered them five to one. Victory looked futile and the only thing they had going for them was their desire to survive. The leader of the small group decided to execute a very bold plan. He had his men load up on a half dozen ships and sailed over to a nearby island where the enemy had set up camp preparing to attack their people in the morning. Once they landed on this island he commanded his men to destroy the ships so there was no way to return home. He then addressed his men and told them that they were fighting for their right to live. He said that even though they were outnumbered five to one that they would fight until the end. Now that they had destroyed their ships there was no hope or thought of retreat. The only way that they would ever see their homes or family again would be to defeat their enemy. What he had done is cut off any safety net or means of escape. The men knew that the only way they'd live is through victory on the battlefield. They mounted a surprise attack on the larger group and through fierce fighting, triumphed.

Think about the goal that you'd like to attain. How committed are you to attaining it? Have you created several alternative plans that you could fall back on should you fail? If you have then you've already convinced yourself that you won't attain it. You must work toward your goal as if there were no retreat similar to the warriors who were fighting for their lives. You don't need to be destitute to begin with, but you do need to have the same hunger as if you were.

Having goals also gives you hope. With goals you have something positive to look forward to each day. With goals you have direction in your life and know what you need to do. Goals create excitement and happiness as you see yourself moving towards them. People who don't have goals or things to look forward to often find themselves in a rut or going nowhere. It's as if their lives were spiraling downward and they have no idea how to change it. This in turn can lead to sadness, depression, extreme anxiety and a long list of various disorders.

TIP: "Goals" are the key to getting you on the track to happiness, health and wealth. Once you have clear defined goals you know exactly what your next step needs to be. You have a destination that you can now work towards. You are no longer spinning your wheels traveling in circles. You know where you're going.

HOW TO CHOOSE GOALS

The first step in deciding what goal to choose is to make an assessment of your present situation. Are you happy with your life exactly the way it is right now? If not is there anything you'd like to change in the areas of health, wealth, relationships or any other area of your life?

"Are you happy with your life exactly the way it is right now?"

You'll learn two exercises in this section on how to decide upon your goals. It's important to realize that there are both short-term and long-term goals. By choosing both short and long-term goals you can better direct your life towards the progress that you desire. Where would you like to see yourself one year from now? How would you like your life to be different one year from now? For long-term goals ask yourself where you'd like to see yourself 10 years from now? It's helpful to have both long and short-term goals that you're working towards. The short-term goals can be steps towards attaining your long-term ones.

TWO CONSIDERATIONS BEFORE CHOOSING A GOAL

Will I Enjoy the Goal? - Will the end result be worth it? If your goal is a new career, will you enjoy doing this type of work once you get it? Remember the purpose of life is to be happy so any goal that you choose should also make you happy?

Will I Enjoy the Trip? - Some goals may require months or even years to attain them. They may also require many different steps or tasks to be accomplished. Your life's happening right now. This is the most important time that you have. Are you enjoying the journey to your goal? Are the tasks and knowing that it will take so long worth it? If you don't enjoy the journey then the destination really doesn't matter.

Exercise #1: Choosing your Goals

Make a list of everything you'd like to accomplish, to have, to be or to attain. Allow your imagination to run free. When you create this list of how you'd like to be, think of it as if you're a writer and it's a Fairy Tale life. A life where anything's possible and you can do or have anything imaginable. Don't worry at this point if any of your responses sound silly or are what you'd even consider unattainable. Write down everything that you'd like to improve or increase upon. Once you've created that list, prioritize it in order of importance.

By participating in this exercise you'll be able to write down the things that you really want without restrictions or limitations. What's your ideal job or what would you like to have as a career? What would your ideal relationship be like? What would your ideal home look like? Where would you like to travel? Just take some time and allow your imagination to have fun with the idea. Then make your list.

_____

_____

_____

_____

_____

_____

_____

Exercise #2: Law of Polarity

Before you go on further making plans with your list take a moment to complete this list as well. You may be very surprised what you learn about yourself. Use the form below and imagine a line down the center from top to bottom creating equal sides. Now make a list in the left column of all the things that you don't want for yourself or in your life.

It's important that you do this list fairly quickly without dwelling on the things that you don't want. Once you've finished this list, on the right side you will write the polarity of each item. Polarity means the *exact opposite*. So if on the left side you wrote something similar to, "I don't want to keep arguing with my spouse." On the right side you would write something like, "I want to have a wonderful relationship with my spouse." Or "I want to be more loving, caring or extremely happy with my relationship."

What I Do Not Want   -   Polarity *(opposite)*

_____

_____

_____

_____

_____

_____

_____

Once you've taken the time to complete this exercise, look at all of the things you've written in Exercise #1 and compare them with the list on the right column of Exercise #2. Do they look the same? Many times the list in Exercise #2 will include more of the important things in life rather than just material things. Once you've compared these lists you can prioritize them by importance. Take a moment to decide which one you'd like to work on first.

7 STEP GOAL FORMULA

Now that you've decided on what your goal is, it's important to make sure that your goal conforms to all of the steps within the goal formula described in this chapter.

Once you understand and learn how to use this formula to create and attain your personal goals you'll also be able to use it to set:

> Professional goals
> Spiritual goals
> Family goals
> Health goals
> Relationship goals
> or any other kind of goals you can imagine.

"A Formula always works regardless of what is fed into it!"

 TECHNICAL STUFF: *A Formula* is a scientific equation that always works. An example would be if you know how to multiply 3 x 3 then you can replace those numbers with any other equations and be able to easily complete the multiplication because you know the formula. That's what makes it a formula; it always works no matter what's fed into it.

STEP ONE: Identify what you want and write it down.

You must have a detailed step-by-step description of exactly what it is you're planning on accomplishing and how you wish to accomplish it. Have you really taken the time to completely think through your goal? You may find that to plan your goal properly it may take several hours to an entire day. It's important not to rush it so you can take the time to be as clear and precise as possible to what you really want.

Once you're ready to define your goal, it's important to take the time to write it down clearly on paper. There's a major difference between typing your goal and writing it out by hand. The art of writing it out personalizes your goal and helps you to ensure that it's mentally accepted. Writing things is also a form of suggestion that allows you to use your imagination and begin the process of imprinting the goal within your subconscious mind through the use of your strong imagination.

STEP TWO: Why do you want this goal?

That is a very important question to ask. Why do you want to accomplish the task that you're setting forth? What's the purpose of it and what's the benefit? More importantly how will your goal benefit you? If it's not going to benefit you in any way then what's your motivation? The most important person in your life should be you. Be sure to make yourself happy.

STEP THREE: Identify the obstacles you must overcome.

Are there any obstacles that immediately stand in your way that can be eliminated or dealt with? Be sure to identify and address all of your obstacles. It's important to take care of them properly rather than simply ignoring them. Ignoring obstacles or hindrances won't make them go away. Proof of that point would be to try and ignore the police officer at your window the next time you get stopped for speeding. How do you plan on dealing with each one of the obstacles?

STEP FOUR: List the people, groups, materials or things required.

What do you think you'll need in the area of assistance or anything outside of your control such as materials, professional help or specialized equipment?

If your goal requires starting a new business will you require any equipment, stock, employees or other materials to begin? Does it require renting a building, office or warehouse space? Is there paperwork, a computer or books required to research?

In the case of starting a business you may need assistance in the way of an accountant, business attorney or possibly approval from city councilmen, code enforcement officers or law enforcement officials.

Will you need assistance from friends, relatives or neighbors in order to attain your goal? Will you have to hire plumbers, carpenters, contractors, electricians, food service personnel, caterers, maintenance people or instructors to attain your goal?

STEP FIVE: What type of knowledge is required?

Will you require any specialized knowledge in order to attain your goal? Should you take some correspondence or online courses? Should you attend a community college or trade school? Are there any licensing or preliminary requirements required to attain your goal? Do you have to be in a certain area to attain your goal?

If your goal requires specialized knowledge that you don't have and aren't able to attain reasonably; where can you get this knowledge? Can you hire someone who has this knowledge? Can this knowledge be attained online or by a professor at a local college? Be sure to know what knowledge you'll require and where you're able to obtain it.

STEP SIX: Create a plan of action to reach your goal.

Create a detailed plan of everything that must be done to attain your goal. In order for anything to happen you must begin by taking action. The difference between success and failure is *taking action*. What are you doing about it? You may have heard many people in the past say the saying, "God helps those who help themselves." In other words while creative imagination is a major step in the right direction, action must be taken towards attaining your goals as well. I remember a slogan from my old *Sunday School* days which stated; "Faith without works is dead." (James 2:26). You must create an action plan and then execute that plan.

STEP SEVEN: Deadlines and Reporting

> *"A goal is a dream with a deadline."*
> Napoleon Hill

Set dates as to when you expect to accomplish various parts of your goal. If it's a big goal you may want to break it down in smaller portions having several dates set up in increments along the way. Remember your goal has to be believable in order to be attainable so breaking it down into believable portions can be the difference between success and failure. The Buddhist monks have a saying that states, *"The journey of 1000 miles starts with the first step."*

Reporting is a vital step in the process of success. This is one of the steps that's *usually missing* in most goals that fail. It's important to find someone who can help you in attaining your goals by being the person that you report to on a periodic basis to show your progress and to ensure that you meet your deadlines. They can also be used as a sounding board should you run into any snags along the way. If you have not attained your deadlines upon reporting time, this person can also help you to reset new, attainable ones.

You may be able to find a work partner for a business goal and in the case of a personal goal maybe you can find a friend or family member. Be sure that this person is someone who is positive minded and will encourage you to attain your goal. Their job will also be to encourage you to try harder should you miss your deadlines.

"You may want to consider soliciting the help of a professional success or life coach."

You may want to consider soliciting the help of a professional success or life coach. They're trained to assist you in taking your goal and breaking them down into smaller steps that are easily attainable. They can encourage and guide you through the process of attaining them and are there throughout the process for guidance, follow through and reporting. They can be as helpful to attaining personal success as having a sports coach is to a professional football team. Have you ever seen a football team make it to the Super Bowl without a coach? It's the coaching that guided them and kept them on track to attaining their goal.

In my earlier years as a clinical hypnotherapist I used to conduct single session smoking cessation programs. I found that in most instances when the client didn't return to my office for a second appointment it was much easier for them to start smoking again. Later on I went to a four-week smoking cessation program where the client would quit smoking on the first day but return for follow-up sessions each week. During the week they had assignments to complete that would keep them on track. As a result of this new program I found that when the clients returned to my office, if they accomplished their assignments they stayed on track.

Occasionally they'd call and tell me that they weren't able to attend one or two of the sessions and invariably they'd begin smoking again. As a result of observing this for many years I realized that the process of reporting progress to someone else keeps goals on track and in alignment.

> *"The process of reporting progress to someone else keeps your goals on track."*

THE STATEMENT OF INTENT

Now that you've created your goal and put it through the Goal Formula it's important to create a clear statement of intent from it.

TECHNICAL STUFF: *A statement of intent* is designed to assist you in utilizing your imagination to attract and accomplish your goal by participating in exercises where you can successfully imagine yourself as already having accomplished your goal.

In order to attract your goal you must convince your mind that you've already accomplished it through imagining that you've done so. The theory here as mentioned before is *that the subconscious mind doesn't understand the difference between an imagined memory and a real one.* By practicing this step repetitively your subconscious mind will eventually accept the imagined memory as a real one and make it so.

A LETTER TO SANTA

In addition to being as imaginative as possible your Statement of Intent must be written in a coherent nature. The reason for this is that the more you can keep the thoughts of what you want in your mind, the more you'll dwell upon it. It's this constant dwelling and desire that attracts the item to you. A coherent statement will help you to fix your focus.

If you were going to send a letter to a friend you'd not just send the entire alphabet written in random order hoping they'd put it together nor would you send a few random words. You'd send a coherent message that would make sense so they'd know exactly what you wanted without any misunderstandings. You'd be detailed, precise and to the point. It works the same way in creating your statement.

If you wanted a new car for instance, if you simply asked for a car how would the Universe know how to fill you order? What type of car, model, year, color, make etc? Try for a moment to fix your attention on a car. By doing that your mind thinks about one car, then another and another. It's all over the place. Did you want a real car, a toy car, a rental car, a car for personal use or a car for work? If you don't know what you want how will the universe? Now imagine that what you wanted was a white, 2018, Lincoln Town Car with gold trim. Can you see how clear the image is now? It's precise and to the point. There's not room for misunderstanding or sending you something that you really didn't want.

I think when it comes to writing a clear Statement of Intent we can learn the most from children. If you've ever seen a child's letter to Santa asking for what they want for Christmas you'd see an expert at work. Here's an example...

Dear Santa,

What I'd really like for Christmas is a New Huffy Rock-it bike. It's the one with the blue handlebars and red frame. It has 12-inch wheels with bright yellow rims and one speed. It also comes with black, 4 inch training wheels which I'll use until I get used to it. It's really shiny and takes less than an hour to assemble. By the way, it says Rockit and HUFFY in big white letters on the frame too. I saw it at Wal-Mart if you have a hard time finding one.

I've been practicing on my friends bike and am getting really good at it. I'd like to use it to go to school and run errands with my brother too. I even cleaned out a space in the garage for it so it will be safe when I'm not using it.

Thank you and have a safe flight,

Love Tommy

From now until Tommy gets his bike it will be very easy for him to keep the picture of it in his imagination as he spelled it out in detail in his letter to Santa. This is the advantage of writing your Statement of Intent in a letter format.

Exercise: Take a moment now to review everything in this chapter, get your thoughts organized and write your Letter to Santa. The letter has already been started with the first three words. You continue from there… *(Be detailed!)*

Dear Santa,

I would like

_____

_____

_____

_____

_____

_____

_____

_____

_____

_____

I've been a good boy / girl,

Thank you.

Your Signature

By the way, even if you haven't been a good boy or girl the process will still work for you, so give it a go. Once you've created your letter to Santa you can eliminate the entire Santa connotation if you like. It's just a means to help you to understand the process more clearly. I think you'll find that the content you've developed will be detailed and sound.

PLACE YOUR ORDER

You've created your statement of intent. The next step is to place your order. You must memorize your statement of intent and recite it to yourself a minimum of twice a day, preferably in the morning when you get up and the second time just before you go to bed. By doing this just before you go to bed your subconscious mind will be able to reflect on it throughout the evening greatly enhancing its power. When you're reciting the statement in your mind it's important to use your imagination and imagine yourself as already having accomplished the goal that you're reading. As you begin reciting it the words may become fragmented and eventually forgotten but as long as you're using your imagination you'll have the basic picture in your mind, which is the most important part.

It's especially effective if you do the reciting of your statement during your quiet time when you're meditating. The quiet time that you've set aside will help you to better imagine the goal that you've set forth for yourself.

> *"Ask and it will be given you."*
>
> Luke 11:9

This "placing your order" process is a vital part of attaining your goals. Without placing your order it would be similar to being in a restaurant with a menu in front of you, knowing what you want to order but never telling anyone. If you've gone through the process of going to the restaurant, reading through the menu, and knowing what you want, then the simplest part of the entire process should be placing your order. It's the same with your goal. You've already done all your homework of deciding what you want and creating your detailed statement of intent including all the previous steps. You have a burning desire to attain your goal. Now, ask for it!

Be emotional: Your attitude determines your altitude. Emotions are among the highest vibrations available to man. By attaching positive emotions to your creative imagination you're greatly accelerating the process.

POWER OF EMOTION

"Your wish is my command."

People are placing orders with the universe or submitting their desires on a constant basis but often times find that they're not receiving what they're asking for. Why is that?

"If the universe is like an Out-of-Control Genie that grants every wish then why are so many wishes not granted?"

The reason for that is that the universe will grant every order that you place however when placing an order it must not be done strictly verbally. Verbal orders are very seldom granted unless their emotional/spiritual counterpart accompanies them. The verbal goal or *statement of intent* must be in emotional harmony with the person placing the order.

(Notice how the Universe grants wishes just like the superconscious mind does, which we spoke of in an earlier chapter. Here's a BIG Newsflash for you... They are alike! In fact both are Source.)

Here is an important secret to understand.

The universe is constantly filling your orders all the time. Everything that's you ask for is always granted. By placing your thoughts, focus and attention on a certain item you're attracting that item whether it's positive or negative.

"It's the actual process of placing your thoughts, focus and attention on something that places the order. Not the actual verbiage or process of repeating the request."

Understanding this concept or secret will help you to understand ɪow you're being granted your wishes continually day and night whether you want them or not. Consider it a vibrational Genie that ɪannot help himself. This is a process which is always happening. Whenever you place your focus on something you want it's being ɪranted. Whenever you place your focus on something you don't want, ɪou're also attracting the exact thing you "don't" want.

ALIGNMENT WITH GOALS

Throughout reading this book keep in mind that your emotions must ɪe in alignment with whatever you desire. Also keep in mind that ɪositive, good feelings mean that you are in alignment with your inner ɪource or Subconscious. Negative emotions mean that you are not in ɪlignment. Always strive to have positive emotions in order to be ɪccessful and progress. To sum up this entire section on emotion, in ɪder to be happy in life; "feel happy".

LIFESTYLE ALIGNMENT

Are you presently living in alignment with the type of lifestyle that you desire? Are you prepared to accept what you desire? Take a moment to think about that. Many people will say, "I want to be a billionaire." I think that's great but if that's the case are you living in alignment with being a billionaire? Here are some examples: Where do you go when you go out to eat? What hotels do you stay at when you travel? What kind of car are you driving? What pastimes do you enjoy? Now that you have answered these questions see if they're in alignment with what you want. If not then you may want to make some changes.

If you want to be rich do you eat at 5 star restaurants or McDonalds?
Do you stay at the Ritz or Motel 6?
Are you driving a Mercedes or an old Ford Escort?
Do you prefer the symphony or mud wrestling?
Do you frequent country clubs or strip clubs?

Granted, not everyone reading this book has a Mercedes already but where is your frame of mind? If you had the money, would you want one? If not then maybe that's not the lifestyle you should be pursuing. That's the purpose of making a clear statement of intent. Lots of people really haven't taken the time to think about what they want and once they do, once they really break it down to the details, many times they change their mind and realize that's not what they really wanted after all.

There are many levels of alignment in all areas of success. Do you know if you're living in alignment with your true desires right now? Would you like to find out? Read the following exercise and actually do it! Yes that means you will have to write in the book. It's okay, it's yours and you can do it. *(Unless you borrowed it from a friend.)*

Alignment Exercise:

In the following categories, on a scale of 1 – 6 *(6 being the highest)* where would you rank your level of alignment? Choose your level of alignment right now, date it and compare it a few weeks later with your new level of alignment then. This is a great gauge to see your progress.

Financial Success: (circle one) Today's date:
_____

      6. A billionaire?
      5. A millionaire?
      4. A thousandaire?
      3. A few bucks here and there?
      2. A red-liner?
      1. Way in the hole?

Health Success: Today's date: _____

      6. Perfect health?
      5. Minor disorders occasionally?
      4. Monthly Doctor visits?
      3. Less than 15 pills a day?
      2. Usually sick?
      1. Sick and tired of being sick?

Relationship Success: Today's date: _____

      6. Partners and happiness in all things?
      5. Good relationships?
      4. Getting along usually?
      3. Tolerating each other?
      2. Constantly arguing?
      1. Searching for my next X relationship?

If what you're in alignment with now isn't what you want, then now's the time to change it. When you imagine yourself successful, see yourself as already having attained your goal and you'll begin attracting it to you.

Once you've chosen your goals and are actively on the path of working towards them return here and complete this exercise again.

RIGHT SPEECH

It's very important to be constantly vigilant in guarding your speech and thoughts. Remember the saying, *"You are what you think about most of the time."* Your words come from your thoughts and once you say them you dwell on them even more. In addition to that, others will dwell on what you say as well. So your words can either be very healing or poisonous.

Speak only of truth rather than appearances. Just as there's right thought you should also practice right speech. Never speak of yourself, what you're doing or anything else in a negative or discouraging way. Everything about your situation in life is great. It's absolutely wonderful in fact. There's no such thing as failure. There's only success in everything you do.

Never speak of how things are hard, how the economy is bad, how your business is slow, your financial problems or the competition is hurting you. Never mention that you didn't have a chance to progress or how things are unfair. None of that exist in your world. There's no competition for you. There's only creativeness. When you compete you're fighting with someone else for a limited amount of their business. That's why there's competition. You both want the same thing. When you are creative you go beyond that limited amount of business that the other guy has and you're open to limitless possibilities. The economy is great and there's never been a better time to be on this earth or to be in business than now.

Train yourself to look at the world as something that is always becoming better. See the silver lining in all things. In every situation no matter how bad there's always something good to be found in it. After the fiercest of forest fires, new green sprouts begin and a lush new forest appears that's even better than the last one. Look at the end of things or even failures as the beginning of new opportunities. Be patient and wait for your goals to appear. If they don't come when you expect them then still be patient as something even better may occur.

The universe will always reward you in ways that you can't imagine. Therefore if you don't get what you expect, be patient and realize that it will be so much better when it arrives. After all if you got exactly what you expected then it didn't come from the universe but from your own efforts because "you" expected it. If it were from the universe it would have been out of the ordinary or beyond your expectations.

Put the past behind you. Its lessons have already been given. It's time to leave the past and move ahead. Expect advancement in all that you do. Even Jesus speaks of leaving the past behind when he says, "Let the dead bury their dead." Rather than holding onto grudges and anger for people in your past, Let GO! The people who delivered messages or lessons in your past, whether they were positive, negative even painful, were only the messengers. It's the message that you had to deal with and learn from. That's all that mattered. The messenger was not important. If it hadn't been them it would have been someone else delivering it. "Don't shoot the messenger. Let go the past, turn around, move ahead and don't look back. It's over and the future is now beginning.

When speaking of how poor you or your family were when you were growing up or the difficult life you had, or the sicknesses or infirmities you overcame, you're only hurting yourself. Don't do it. By focusing on the negativity of your past you're drawing more of that negativity to you. You're classifying yourself as a poor or destitute type of person. Leave all things pertaining to poverty, hardship, negative upbringing, broken homes and hunger behind you. There's nothing good those memories can do for you in your future. By letting them go you'll have added strength and momentum to move ahead as you focus on the attaining of health, wealth and happiness.

LIVE BIGGER THAN LIFE

Are you truly ready to receive the abundance you're asking for? You can only advance if you're bigger than your situation.

If you want more money you must be bigger than who you've been. If you want a better job you must be bigger than the one you have.

If you have 50 gallons of water and tried to pour it into a one gallon container what would happen? 49 gallons of water would be lost, wasted and gone. Why would anyone want to give you the additional 49 gallons if they knew it would just be wasted? That would be crazy. In order to have more of anything you must grow.

This is very similar in our lives. Whatever we find to be our comfort level, we'll be filled with abundance to that level. Water seek its level and then overflows. So does abundance. The more you grow the more you can accept. If you want a better job, be bigger than the one you now have and you will be promoted; if not by your present boss then by the Universe itself. It's a universal rule. As you *grow* you are *filled* with more. How often do you notice people who are well educated, excited, energetic, ambitious and goal oriented who are unemployed for long or working in public service jobs? They're bigg than those positions and receive more.

Think of some of the most successful people in the nation. Donald Trump, Anthony Robbins, Oprah Winfrey and Joel Osteen just to name a few. What do they all have in common? They're all bigger than life. No way could they be working a meager job, destitute or penniless. Their vessels are huge and filled with abundance from the Universe to accommodate them. Instead of being satisfied with being a big fish in a small pond they are big fish in a big pond.

If you live big, act big and expect big, you'll be rewarded big. It's a law of nature and it's that simple. How big is your container? One gallon, 10 gallons or a thousand gallons?

Did you realize that the majority of people that won the lottery have spent it or are broke inside of a year again? Why's that? They didn't expand or grow. You cannot pour more money into a person than he can contain or it will spill over and be lost. If you want more of anything, money, a promotion, health or other types of abundance all you need to do is grow. Be positive, think big and move ahead. You must become bigger than your present container.

ACT AS IF YOU ALREADY HAVE IT

> *"By thought, the thing you want is brought to you;*
> *by action you receive it."*
> Wallace Wattles

You must imagine that you have already attained your goal in order for your subconscious mind to accept it as a memory. It will draw it to you much quicker. By acting like you have accomplished it already you're actually *living in alignment* with the goal. Remember you cannot attract anything that you're not in alignment with. A frequency being sent out at 97.5 can only be received by someone tuned in to 97.5. You must be an alignment with what you are attracting.

RIGHT ACTION

This is the third part of the triad. Right thought, right speech and now right action. This is not new by the way. Buddhist Monks have been practicing these three principles for years. Simply put, right action is to act the way you want to act rather than the way society or appearances expect you to act. It's to act as if you "already have" what it is you're working towards attaining.

I was watching a documentary a while back where a college girl decided to conduct an experiment at her college to see how she would be treated if she were to dress differently. She decided to dress professionally from that point forward. She went to classes and everywhere else dressed in smart looking business suits. Some of her day was recorded on video so the viewers could see the difference between the way she dresses and the dress of the others in class. Most were in jeans and t-shirts.

She had related how before the experiment hardly anyone paid attention to her, including her teachers. After only a few days things began to change drastically. She found that many of her classmates were coming to her to ask for advice on their schoolwork, careers and even personal life. They suddenly began to look up to her as someone who was in authority and more knowledgeable. Even the instructors began to notice her more. She noted that the instructors would all make a point of greeting her individually when she entered the classroom and would frequently call upon her for answers and confirmation. They had hardly ever called on her before. You can see how simply "acting" professional resulted in everyone treating her professional.

> **THOUGHTS:** This is a *five-word formula for right action* that can change your life in any area you desire.
>
> "To be _____, act _____."
> *(Fill in the blanks with whatever you would like to change or be in your life)*
>
> *Here are some examples:*
>   To be happy act happy.
>   To be sad act sad.
>   To be healthy act healthy.
>   To be sick act sick.
>   To be wealthy act wealthy.
>   To be poor act poor.

Here's an exercise to prove my point:

If you are serious about creating effective change in your life, I'd like you to "really" get up and do this exercise!

Exercise:
1. Stand up in front of a mirror and look at yourself.
2. Put your chest out, shoulders back and head up high.
3. Give yourself a big smile and keep it there.
4. Now, while keeping this pose, try to be sad or depressed. You can't!

You're acting like you're very happy and that's how you feel. You may have even laughed while in this position. If you acted the opposite however you'd feel the opposite as well but please don't do that as I want you to feel good about what you're learning rather than the alternative.

GRATITUDE - THE KEY TO ELEVATE ABUNDANCE

Showing gratitude towards your goal as if you've already attained it will also greatly tip the scales towards attaining your desires. By having an attitude of gratitude while imagining your statement of intent, the universe will give you more of what you're in alignment with. Being grateful for what you're working on will help you convince your subconscious that you've already attained it thereby making it happen.

Keep in mind that there are people who are doing everything that they should be doing to attain abundance but are still kept in poverty due to their lack of gratitude. When you dwell on poverty or dissatisfaction you're attracting and allowing yourself to be surrounded with poverty. Dissatisfaction and gratefulness are at opposite ends of the spectrum.

"Your abundance will be in direct proportion
to your service and gratitude."

In the section on Right Action you were taught to Act as if you've already attained whatever it is you desired. You should also be grateful for whatever it is you desire as if you already have it. Yes, even if you don't have it yet. If you're grateful as if you do have it, you'll be drawing it to you with much more force.

Gratefulness Exercise:

On the next page you'll make a list of what you're grateful for that you now have. Be as detailed as possible and put as many things as you can think of. Include everything pertaining to health, abundance, relationships, happiness, items and opportunities etc.

Once you've completed that list continue adding to it by listing all the things that you'd like to have in your life. These are the things you are presently working towards (your goals) that you're grateful for. Write them as if you already have them.

Remember to make them as spectacular as you can. The more excitement you can create in the list the better it will be for you. Always look at your thankful items in the present tense as much as possible.

GREATFUL LIST

Keep this list handy and review it each morning when you get up and as often during the day as you have time for. Take a moment to imagine each one while being thankful for it. Be as emotional as possible. You'll find that the most convenient place to keep your Grateful List is in this book.

I AM GREATFUL FOR:

_____

_____

_____

_____

_____

_____

E

GREATFUL LIST CONTINUED

_____

_____

_____

_____

_____

_____

_____

_____

_____

_____

_____

_____

_____

_____

_____

_____

_____

_____

GREATFUL LIST CONTINUED

_____

_____

_____

_____

_____

_____

_____

_____

_____

_____

_____

_____

_____

_____

_____

_____

_____

_____

SERVICE INSIDE YOUR FIELD
Why Service

How much do you really want to attain your goal? What would you be willing to do in return for it? Would you be able to teach or help other people to do what you did? Does your goal include anything that could benefit others?

It's important if you wish to receive assistance from the universe that your goal is expansive and in some way benefits mankind. If you were building a solar powered automobile for instance it would benefit society as they would be able to use it and save money as well as energy. This goal would also help nature by using a clean form of energy. If your goal were to have a happier relationship, that would help others as well. With a happier relationship you'd be more pleasant. It would also be more pleasant for other people to be around you. It would create a happier household and possibly even work environment.

IMPORTANT: It's said that if you want to truly learn something, *teach it.* That's especially true with any goals that you want to attain. If you want to learn how to make money, then teach others the best way to do it. In order to teach other people you'll have to learn as much as possible to be an authority in your field. The more that you teach the better you'll be. Once you get to the point where you can help others to be successful, so will you be.

If you're unhappy with your present rewards or your income, all yo have to do is increase your contributions or service.

> *"As ye sow, so shall ye reap."*
> Marcus T. Cicero

If you're in an occupation presently that helps, teaches or enhances people in any way perhaps the best way you can be of service is through your own occupation. Perhaps you'd want to teach at the local continuing education program in your city. If you're a counselor for instances it may be more beneficial to help others with your talent rather than to work in a soup kitchen for the day. How can you be of the most service?

Another idea is to simply give things of value to the public that can help them. One of the ways that I've been blessed to help thousands of people in the area of hypnosis and self-help is by "giving away" our Clinical Hypnosis Manual, which is the current curriculum for our schools worldwide. People thought I was crazy for doing this initially but the benefit of giving away the manual has far surpassed what I had imagined. The manual has helped thousands of people who were new to hypnosis and many that would have never had the chance to learn what they were capable of. They were able to help themselves, their friends and loved ones with a variety of issues such as smoking cessation, stress and weight loss just to name a few. It has also helped many seasoned hypnosis practitioners to upgrade their knowledge to current and advanced procedures.

As a result of assisting the universe in its purpose of expanding I've been blessed in countless ways to include increased income, a much larger influence on the Internet, grateful new friends internationally as well as many interesting opportunities and offers.

How else can you be of service in your business? What can you do that will give your client more in product value or service than you're receiving in cash value? If you sell an ice cube to an Eskimo in Alaska that wouldn't benefit them very much but if you sold it to someone in the Arizona Dessert it would have a great value to them. How can you truly help others in what you already do?

SERVICE OUTSIDE YOUR FIELD

Where should you be of service? How should you be of service? What should you do? These are all very good questions that only you can answer. I'll however leave you some guidelines that you may find helpful in your decision-making process.

There are many ways of being of service. You can help individuals within the same field of study that you are in. You may decide to help groups of many people at once. You may decide to go outside of your field altogether and work with organized charities or fundraisers. Each one of these are worthwhile causes.

When deciding who to work with or donate your talents or income, take a moment to establish what this organization or group is in alignment with. Look at the purpose of the group and their focus. When you think about the group, where are you placing your thoughts, focus and attention? What's being drawn to you? Are they an organization that's working towards the attracting of something positive or are they an organization fighting something negative? An example of this would be "The War on Terrorism". Compared to; "The March for Peace." Take a moment to think about those two titles. When repeating the first one, where are you placing your thoughts, focus and attention? What's being attracted, more terrorism? When looking at the second group it's obvious that what you're attracting is peace.

It's important to only work with an organization that's attracting something positive rather than negative. Even though the ultimate cause may be good, when you have a title such as the fight against cancer, the fight against AIDS or the fight against diabetes, what do they seem to be attracting? More of what they're fighting against and the sad thing is that most of them are clueless to what they're doing.

Even Mother Theresa during an interview stated that she wouldn't be part of an organization that was fighting against something such as war, hatred or terror. However she did say if there was a movement towards peace; that she would gladly endorse it.

So keep these things in mind when you're looking for someplace to be of service. In the long run are you helping the universe in its purpose of increase or are you being part of the problem?

HOW TO GIVE

I'd like to leave you with one last thought that I feel is very important on being of service. The attitude that you hold in being of service is extremely important. Are you being of service because you actually want to help people or are you doing it only to get ahead yourself? It's important that you do this for the right reason and that your heart is in the right place. Keep in mind that your subconscious mind and the Universal Consciousness are one and the same. So if you think you're trying to *get over* or *fool* anyone, the joke's on you...

> *"Your subconscious knows what you're doing*
> *and why you're doing it even before you begin."*

Be sincere in all your endeavors. If you're going to be of service, do it out of caring and love. Enjoy doing it. There are many benefits to helping others besides money such as satisfaction, appreciation and being useful. Remember the old saying, "What goes around comes around."

THE UNIVERSAL PROMISE

By being of service to others you're assisting the Universe in its ultimate purpose, which is to increase. The more that you can help others to increase the more you'll be blessed or rewarded from the Universe. While you're being of service to others, you can also *show them how to serve others* as well. That will greatly magnify the whole purpose of increasing. You'll find that the universe will reward you in an amount that can often times be more than you're prepared to receive. Therefore as you're preparing your plan of being of service to others also prepare yourself for increase.

"You can have anything you want if you want it badly enough. You can be anything you want to be, do anything you set out to accomplish if you hold to that desire with a singleness of purpose."

Abraham Lincoln

REMEMBER:

1. Without goals you'll travel aimlessly through life.

2. A person with clear defined goal can't be depressed.

3. Your Statement of Intent must be written in coherent sentences.

4. You must first "place your order" to receive it.

5. Prepare to receive your order.

6. Be patient and never give up when waiting for completion.

7. The journey is equally as important as the goal. You should enjoy them both.

8. Emotion supercharges your order.

9. Be in alignment with your goal.

10. Live your life as if you've already attained your goal.

11. Be grateful for all that you have.

12. Be bigger than life to progress. You must outgrow your present situation.

13. Offer more in service that giving in cash value.

14. The universe promises to reward all those who assist in its purpose of expansion in ways that they cannot imagine.

CHAPTER 7

PERMANENT HABIT
CREATION

"The world cries out for the teachers
who can teach their hearers
the true science of abundant life."

Wallace D. Wattles

THE MISSING INGREDIENT

There are countless programs available on the market today including self-help CDs, books, seminars, television programs, workshops and the list goes on. One thing they all have in common is that they'll all help you to progress and feel great for a *short time*. Within a few days however it seems that people revert to how they were before they began these programs. Why hasn't the change become permanent? What's missing? The missing ingredient is *habit creation*. In order to maintain any positive change it must become a habit. Once you've created a habit it then becomes part of your self-image.

> *"The missing ingredient is habit creation."*

Take a moment to think of the many habits that you have right now. In order for them to become second nature, for you to be able to complete them without thinking of them consciously you had to go through a stage of repetition. For example, the habit of driving to work each day without even thinking took more than one day to accomplish. It may have even taken a month or two before you were able to drive there in an *"automatic pilot"* type of mindset.

Even people who developed the habit of smoking reported that they had initially found it distasteful. In the beginning they would cough each time they inhaled. Then they learned to not inhale as deeply until they were able to get past the hurdle of breathing in smoke. They found the taste undesirable and the feeling of the smoke going into their nose agitating. However through repetition and determination they were able to continue smoking without a problem and eventually even enjoyed the process.

Another example would be going to the gym. Developing a habit to go to the gym each day requires getting up earlier or setting aside extra time that you would have normally used for something else. Keeping hat specific time open for the purpose of going to the gym alone was a major hurdle to get over. In addition to that, you had to make sure that you had enough rest to be able to perform the task that you were going here for. Once you began working-out at the gym the muscles of your body began to hurt since they weren't used this way in such a long ime. Through repetition, eventually everything became easier, less of a burden, a routine and eventually an enjoyable occurrence.

In each of these instances the habit had been created over time. It ook conscious action, repetition and persistence to succeed. This is the ame process that it will take to develop any habit in the future as well. 's amazing how some people who have developed a habit of smoking or 20 to 30 years think that they can actually develop a habit of being a on-smoker in a one-hour session. It's as if people are looking for the *"magic spell"* or *"quick fix"* that will immediately change them. You an accomplish anything that you set your mind to; however if you ant it to stick you must create a permanent habit through repetition.

REATE A HABIT BY HABIT

> **TECHINAL STUFF:** *A habit* is defined as a pattern of behavior that often occurs gradually and automatically. The continual repetition of any behavior, good or bad can ultimately create a habit. The results of these subconscious habits are a major determining factor in one's self-image.

That's the essence of a habit. Once a series of actions becomes miliar to you they can begin to operate on their own as a)conscious behavior. They oftentimes aren't even noticed by the nscious mind.

Here are some habits that you may be familiar with. Notice how once you begin them they seem to be accomplished with very little effort.

> Tying your shoelaces
> Having a cigarette immediately after a meal
> Eating popcorn while watching a movie
> Driving to work the same way each day
> Sitting in your favorite chair rather than the one next to it
> Bringing your hands to your face when you sneeze
> Putting on the brakes of your car upon seeing a red light
> Typing without looking at the keys
> Saying *"God bless you"* when someone sneezes
> Reciting the alphabet
> Taking a shower
> Doing the dishes
> Making the bed
> Going through your exercise routine or jogging
> Riding a bicycle
> Sleeping on a certain side of the bed
> Biting your nails
> Brushing your teeth

Although habits can be quite advantageous, the problem is that many negative habits are also created that hinder our growth such as those that create negative belief systems, self-doubt, self-sabotage and lack of follow-through type attitudes. These habits whether negative or positive create our financial, relationship and health blueprints. They determine your perception of reality.

> *"Changing habits have the ability to alter your memories*
> *of the past in alignment with your present reality."*

An earlier chapter explained that memories are not stored in a separate, secure compartment, safe and isolated from everything else in the mind. They reside in the same places that feelings, thoughts and desires are stored. As your goals, habits and feelings change so do your memories so as to act in accordance with them. The memories of each person are perceived so as to reflect their individual current reality.

YOU ARE A SHADOW OF YOUR PRESENT

Right now as you are reading this book you're the result of your past thoughts, feelings and experiences. Another way to put it is that you're actually a shadow person of the "past" you. Everything that you've done in the past has made you the person that you are today. This very moment as you're taking your present breath you're creating a new "future" you.

The most powerful, important and transforming time of your life is in this present moment. Now's all that matters. The past is gone; the future has not been written and right now is when you're writing it. What do you want to create?

"No matter what kind of person you are, regardless of your past, you can change it all right now."

By controlling your thoughts, focus and attention in the areas that you desire you're creating the future you. You're the creator of your own reality and are in charge of your destiny. That's the purpose of reading this book. This is a book of change, an instruction manual for you to create a new and improved future you. It's never too late to change. The first step that's required is action. Every choice that you make right now, no matter how insignificant, determines the direction and quality of your life. Keep in mind that even the greatest oceans of the world were created one drop at a time.

BRAIN BIOLOGY OF HABIT FORMING

Everything that's psychological is also biological at the same time. All of your urges, ideas, thoughts, moods, feelings and desires are biological in nature. Everything that you do requires that you have a body. Try to hold this book without one; I'm sure it would be a difficult task. It seems that people try to separate biological and psychological functions; however one without the other would be impossible. Your physical body is required in order to breathe, eat, think, imagine, pump the blood through your system, learn and anything else you do. It would be similar to having a motor without a vehicle. You simply wouldn't get anywhere.

THE BRAIN

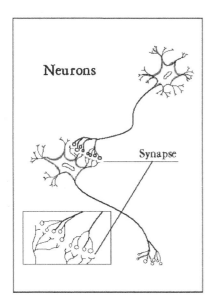

Neurons

Synapse

Habit formation is a process, which is developed in the portion of the brain known as the *basal ganglia*. The *basal ganglia* are an interconnected mass of nuclei located in the forebrain between the cortex and the upper part of the brainstem. This is the part of the brain that's responsible for habit creation and memories. The specific portion of the ganglia attributed to habit creation is known as the striatum.

Within the striatum are a series of billions of neurons, which are creating trillions of neural networks. A remarkable feature of these neurons is that they don't actually touch. There's a small gap between each one, which is known as the synapse. The neurons communicate with each other across these gaps by creating an extremely vast network firing out chemical and electrical signals containing information. This information can be communicated to thousands of neurons simultaneously or to a single neuron at a time. The information that is electrically fired between the synapse areas from one neuron to another is similar to an electrical storm as they travel in a sort of a ricocheting type manner.

Continual repetition of these messages makes it easier for the specific action or thought to be repeated as they begin to create new neural-pathways. Once these new pathways are formed they can't be eliminated. Even when they're no longer in use they'll still remain. This is the essence of an addiction. There's a battle between the conscious mind and the "habitual" unconscious.

A new habit can be created which will in turn create new neural pathways that will replace or overwrite the old habit. Keep in mind that the old habit will not be eliminated though. It's still lurking in the background. It's important that the new habit's continued with so that you don't fall back on the old one *(falling off the wagon)* such as in the case of alcoholism or drug abuse.

As new pathways are created they're similar to creating paths through a grassy field. By walking back and forth over the same route repetitiously you're wearing down the grass all the way to the soil. The path is worn deeper and more pronounced as it's repeatedly used.

Now; if a new path is used more than the old one to the point where it also wears down the grass into the soil even deeper then the new one will become easier to use than the old one. The old one will fade into the background and will probably begin to grow grass once again. It takes approximately three to four weeks to form this new habit. Everyone's brain is uniquely different and some may develop habits more quickly than others but they will definitely form.

THE DOPAMINE INFLUENCE

Dopamine's a hormone and neurotransmitter that occurs in the brain associated with reward seeking behavior. It's usually triggered by the thought of an association with sex, food, drugs, caffeine, humor and many other enjoyable or exciting type activities. Observing patrons in a casino type establishment are a good example of the effect of this raised dopamine level. There's excitement in a casino generated by the thought of alcoholic beverages, the possibility of winning, the environment of smoking, attractive waitresses or waiters, flashing lights and loud music just to name a few.

Research has shown that the firing of dopamine-induced neurons is a great motivation to the success of a newly formed habit. This hypothesis is based on the fact that when a reward is greater than expected the dopamine level increases which in turn motivates its recipient towards the reward.

It's easy to remember events from your past that have this emotional, dopamine effect related to them such as the birth of your child, graduation from high school or college, your wedding day, the day you were promoted at work and even the first day you met your partner. Regardless of how long ago these events may have occurred, due to the emotion that is attached to them they seem to be easily retrieved and described. On the other hand, events that do not have exciting conditions attached can be very difficult to remember such as what you were doing two weeks ago on Thursday at 2:00 in the afternoon.

CHUNKING FOR HABITS

Experiments were conducted at the Massachusetts Institute of Technology in which rats were repeatedly made to run through T-shaped mazes. Upon completion of the proper choice the rats were

ewarded with a piece of chocolate at the end of the maze. This gave
hem added incentive due to the raised dopamine level caused by the
chocolate. In the beginning of these experiments the rats displayed
much brain activity as their decisions to turn right or left were being
made. Over time as the tasks began to become habit, the amount of
rain activity began to decrease. The larger amounts of brain activity
were only noticed at the beginning and the end of the tasks as it had
diminished throughout the duration of the process.

This process is very similar with humans. Once repeated activity
as become a habit, conscious brain activity is only required at the
eginning and ending of the task as it's become grouped together or
therwise known as *"chunked"*. We learn a set of behaviors or habits
ll together as a group or a chunk. This can be noticed while shaving
r brushing your teeth. Once the initial cue was given of turning on the
ater everything else seemed to be a calm, non-conscious habit.
ou're even able to multitask while thinking of other things at the same
ne that you're brushing or shaving.

Another example of this "chunking" behavior can be seen in the
abit of driving to a repeated location such as from home to work. If
u've had the opportunity to travel the same route while driving for
any months then chances are that it's become a habit that doesn't
ve to be thought of very much. Your brain activity would be active
you're leaving your home and approaching the car however due to
e chunking process your brain activity would be much lower
oughout the trip until you arrive at your location. Once leaving your
hicle your brain activity would then increase as you decide what to
next. You may have even noticed that while you are driving to and
m work that you're able to do other things such as planning your
orkday or even having a conversation on your cell phone without any
ficulty. Chunking allows you the opportunity to multitask easily.

In many instances paying too much attention to the details of
ating a habit could lead to the actual destruction or non-forming of

the habit. Its gradual processes that must be slowly learned over a period of time in order to become a habit. Coupled with the strength the dopamine neurons, you're creating a new habit that will be very difficult to break.

> *"Creating a habit through this repetitious manner*
> *utilizing the incentive of rewards in the process,*
> *will make it a much stronger habit than the one it's replacing."*

ZERO GRAVITY TEST - NASA

Catching a ball seems to be child's play for most people. It's seems as automatic as riding a bike or tying your shoe, or is it? Years ago I decided to take up juggling as a hobby and I still enjoy doing it on occasion today. One of the interesting things about juggling is that if you watch the highest point of where the balls arch, you can anticipate where the ball will come down and with practice will be able to catch them and juggle like a pro without even watching your hands. The key is to watch the highest arch of the balls and anticipate.

If you take a moment to think about the process you'll realize how much your subconscious mind is operating and computing many variables without your conscious knowledge. In the case of juggling, your mind automatically computes the effect of gravity on the ball after it has peaked. In addition to gravity, approximately a fraction of a second before the ball reaches your hand, your wrist turns to just the right position to receive the ball and clenches its muscles slightly so as to catch the ball without dropping it and to absorb the thrust. This is remarkable series of mathematical computations that's being done subconsciously and rapidly.

> *"The brain seems to anticipate, compensate and calculate*
> *gravitational acceleration on a natural basis."*

How does your brain do it? According to neuroscientists Joe McIntyre of the College De France, the brain's able to accomplish this task because it contains an internal model of gravity. The brain, he says seems to anticipate, compensate and calculate gravitational acceleration on a natural basis.

Here's his conclusion, which was published recently in the journal *"Nature Neuroscience"*, which is based on an experiment that was conducted in space involving ball catching. Astronauts onboard the space shuttle Columbia were monitored while catching balls in a no-gravity environment which were released from a spring-loaded canon. Once a ball was shot from the cannon it would move in a constant speed as opposed to a constant acceleration similar to how they would be on Earth.

While playing catch the astronauts were fitted with electrodes to measure the electrical activity of their arm muscles. The movements of their arms and hands were tracked with infrared cameras as well.

While in flight, with zero gravity, the astronauts were able to catch the ball even though their timing was a bit off. They reacted to the ball as if they were expecting gravity to propel it faster. Surprisingly the astronauts continued reacting to catching the ball as if they expected gravity to be a variable for a period of approximately 15 days.

At around the 15th day of the experiment the astronauts on board the shuttle were beginning to catch the ball more often. Although the quick over reacting movements of their arms continued, the severity of it grew smaller. Gradually they were able to react to catching the ball more accurately and once again just a fraction of a second before catching the ball their hand would clench in order to absorb the impact.

Once the astronauts returned to Earth they continued the experiment with gravity once again. The astronauts stated that they were amazed at how fast the ball seemed to drop as it came towards them. This time however their minds were able to adapt for the change in gravity much quicker than they did in space. McIntyre and his colleagues believe that given different situations the mind's able to learn to compensate and reevaluate acceleration and gravity. It's as if it's able to remember the choices it had experienced and adapt to choosing which one is appropriate for the situation.

You can see through this experiment how the new habit of catching the ball in a no-gravity environment *"began"* to take root in approximately 15 days. It's also interesting to note that once the habit of catching a ball in zero gravity was no longer needed that the mind was able to go back to the previous habit much quicker.

IMAGINING FREE THROWS

The use of *imagination training*, also known as *sports visualization* to create habits of increased success, plays a key role with many great athletes. In addition to sharpening a player's skills it also increases their confidence and motivation. Research has shown that athletes who consistently imagine themselves performing their physical skills actually create what's known as "muscle memory" which helps them improve significantly when they conduct their specific sport.

Proof of this phenomenon was demonstrated through an experiment conducted by Australian psychologist, Alan Richardson. Richardson chose three groups of students who had never practiced creative visualization or imagination techniques in the past. The students were all chosen at random. The experiment involved practicing free throws with a basketball for a period of twenty days.

The first group practiced completing live free throws with an actual "real" ball. The second group practiced live free throws on the first day and twentieth day only as did the third group. Here's where the difference takes place. The second group didn't perform any additional free throws mentally or physically for the entire experiment between the first and twentieth day. The third group spent twenty minutes each day imagining free throws. If for any reason they missed the shot they were to imagine getting it in the basket on the next throw.

Upon completion of the experiment on the twentieth day the results were computed so that the progress could be compared. The first group, which actually practiced live free throws, improved 24%. The second group that had not practiced at all did not improve at all. The third group which had only physically practice as much as the second group but then practice for twenty minutes each day using their imagination had improved 23%. As a result in his published paper in "Research Quarterly", Richardson wrote that;

> *"The most effective visualization occurs when*
> *the visualizer feels and sees what he is doing."*

In other words the visualizers in the basketball experiment "felt" the ball in their hands and "heard" it bounce, in addition to "seeing" it go through the hoop.

In comparing the results of the first group and the third group you can see that they were only 1% apart. As mentioned earlier in this book the subconscious mind measures actual memories and imagined memories as being the same value. This experiment further validates the power of using your imagination for positive change in your life.

BACKGROUND AND STATISTICS

TECHINAL STUFF: Our research shows that approximately 85% of subjects will "rebel against" and eventually "reject" any suggestion given to them requiring change within 3 to 5 days. Since most people don't remember their dreams, they're not aware of this fighting against the suggestions they received. The other 15% of the public are the ones that are able to experience success easily upon having the desire to change. They're the ones that appear to have very strong will power.

This is why many people who decide to quit smoking will resume smoking again within 3 to 5 days. Or when most people decide to lose weight they do great for a few days and then go back to their old negative habits. What happened is they *rejected* the suggestion to stop smoking or eat healthier and returned to their previous behavior.

WHERE DID THE WHOLE CONCEPT START?

Dr. Maxwell Maltz, a plastic surgeon with New York City Hospitals and author of *"Psycho Cybernetics"* conducted extensive studies on how the mind creates these new neural pathways. He found that when any suggestion was repeatedly given for a minimum of twenty one days in a row these neural pathways would actually reroute themselves and create a new habit that would remain within the subjects mind.

This means that our brain doesn't accept data to change a permanent habit unless it's repeated each day for a "minimum" of twenty-one days *(without missing a day)*. If just one day is missed the process must be restarted or the previous habit will stand a chance of resurfacing again.

It's a simple concept but the key is in keeping with it for at least
thirty days as everyone's mind is as different as fingerprints. Although
twenty one days is the minimum amount of days required, thirty or
more days are preferred. The old habit doesn't leave you; it's simply
replaced or overwritten by the new habit. Old habits are permanent and
cannot be eliminated, they can only be overwritten. The new habit will
need to be reinforced and nurtured to have any chance of survival.

IT'S HABIT MAKING TIME

What habit have you decided that you'd like to work on?

For a new habit or a Personal goal

Do you want to create a new permanent habit of one of your goals
such as health, wealth or happiness? Did you choose something
specifically on your goal worksheet? If you've already chosen a
positive habit or goal then you should pass ahead a few pages to the
section titled STEPS TO CREATING A SUCCESSFUL HABIT

For a new habit to replace an existing one

If not, do you want to use the process to replace a bad or undesirable
habit that you already have with a new positive one? If you're
replacing a bad habit then continue with the next section.

MAKE A LIST OF YOUR BAD HABITS

The following list will help you to better define exactly what it is
you want to do. Make a list of all the habits you'd like to change or
find undesirable. Be honest with yourself and put them all down.
Don't worry; I can't see your book so it's your secret alone. Once

you've completed the list move onto the next exercise so you can prioritize your list.

E

LIST OF HABITS

Make a list of all the habits that you'd like to change.

_____

_____

_____

_____

_____

_____

_____

_____

_____

_____

_____

_____

_____

PRIORTIZE THEM

From the previous list, place the habits here in order of priority that you'd like to work on. Keep in mind that you'll be working on one at a time so which ones are the most vital to change now?

_____

_____

_____

_____

_____

_____

_____

_____

_____

_____

_____

_____

_____

IS IT WORTH THE TIME?

From your priority list that you've just created take a moment to think about the top one. Ask yourself if it's worth taking an entire month to create a new habit to replace the old one. The reason I say that is that it will take a 30 day commitment to replace it. If in that process you decide that this habit's not nearly as important as the second one on your list or number 3 just cannot wait, you'll have just wasted a lot of time.

If you feel that the top one on your list is the most important one and you can give it a 30 day commitment, then lets get started. If not, then find the one on your list that you should get started with and begin there. Remember that your conscious mind is very rebellious to begin with and your subconscious is similar to a 5 year old child. If you try to take on more than one habit at a time in this 30 day process, in addition to the hindrance from your conscious mind you may overwhelm your subconscious as well.

Imagine telling your five year old to take out the trash. He or she will do it happily but if you tell them to take out the trash, feed the dog, make their bed and clean up their room at the same time, they'll become overwhelmed, rebel and probably not get any of them done. It's called "human nature". Be patient, one habit at a time and you'll get there. Remember the Great Wall of China was built only one brick at a time.

WHAT IS YOUR REPLACEMENT?

You've listed your habits and chosen the one to work with now. In order to replace it, you must have something to replace it with. When replacing a habit, make sure you're only replacing it with something good. You always replace bad for good. Not bad for OK or bad for So-So. It's similar to replacing the habit of smoking. Replacing it with water would be great but replacing it with cigars or beer wouldn't work out. According to a 5 year old child *(the subconscious)* if it's okay to have something a little bad then why should it release the habit to begin with?

Once you have your replacement habit to work with or in the case of simply creating a New Habit without replacing another, you're ready to begin. Review the following steps to be sure you are as prepared as possible. Some may not pertain but many of them can be the difference between success or failure.

Once you've done that you're ready to begin programming yourself with whatever form of imagination processing you choose to use such as guided imagery, meditation etc. The concept is to imagine yourself each day as being the end result or already having accomplished the new habit. You're in fact imagining your new habit into existence by creating a new memory of the desired event and rewiring your neural connections.

STEPS TO CREATING A SUCCESSFUL HABIT

Creating new habits require conscious awareness, action and repetition. While you're creating the goal that you'd like to become a habit, be sure to include as many of these steps that are applicable within your process.

Make a 30 Day Commitment - How much do you really want to change? Either you want to change or not. If not then you'll remain same. If you do want to change then change requires that you do something different than you've been doing. This is a program that's proven to work, scientifically and biologically, but it does require effort and follow-through on your part. This brings us right back to the initial question. How much do you really want to change?

*"If you have nothing to lose by trying and a great deal to gain
if successful, by all means try."*
W. Clement Stone

Make it Daily - Do it for Today; let tomorrow take care of itself. Take one step at a time. Once you get through today, be thankful that you accomplished your task for one day. Now, do it for another day. If you continue repeating this process you don't have to worry about the future. Your mind will take care of that for you. All you need to do is to continue with the repetition, not missing a day and your permanent habit will be formed.

Make it Grand - If you're going to go through the process of changing yourself for 30 days, why not go for the gold. When creating your goal, make it something that will be exciting to attain. Make it fun, grand and exceptional. This way you'll have more to look forward to during the process.

Be Persistent - Your goal isn't about how fast you get there, it's simply to get there. Patience, persistence and effort will win every time. The more you can think and imagine your goal the quicker it will occur.

*"Your goal must be a driving force in your life.
The more real that you can make it,
the more real it will become."*

Find a Partner - If it's at all possible to work toward your goal with someone else who has a similar goal you can encourage and motivate each other throughout the process. Keep in mind the slogan, "Behind every successful man is a supportive woman." On occasion this even works vice versa. ☺ The encouragement, dedication and brainpower of two or more are always stronger than one.

Create Triggers - Triggers are simple things that you can do that will help to make your process easier. They're reminders that you have created to keep you consciously aware of your goal. These triggers can include things like creating affirmations and placing them in strategic locations around your house where they'll be easily seen.

You can create an imagination board with pictures of your goals posted on it. Place it somewhere where it can be frequently seen. You may even be able to turn your computer screen into an imagination board by setting your pictures to run automatically as a slide show with your favorite music in the background.

If you're trying to create a habit of going to the gym every morning a good trigger would be to set out your gym clothing and sneakers on a chair so they will be seen when you wake up.

Rewards to Raise Dopamine Levels – Dopamine's a natural hormone, which is produced by the brain that heightens pleasure. It's associated with reward seeking behavior. Any time a reward is associated to a habit-forming behavior, the process of forming that habit will be more enjoyable. If someone were to give you an exciting reward for doing a simple task wouldn't you be more likely to want to do it again? That's the concept.

Create Replacements - Keep in mind that once habits are created, they cannot be eliminated. The only way to change a negative habit is to replace it with a new positive habit. Always replace a negative habit with a positive one. If you replace it with an item that's somewhat better but still of negative origin chances are your mind will return to the original habit. The rule of thumb is replacing bad for good rather than bad for not so bad.

Be Thankful - You always attract what you focus on. This is a *constant rule* that works in every instance. If you're thinking negatively you'll attract negative to you and if you're thinking positively you'll attract positive. Whether you believe in this concept or not you're right either way because you'll draw more of what you believe to you. Being in a state of thankfulness will also make you happier and more pleasant to be around. Thankfulness is contagious.

"If you can keep your mind in a state of thankfulness for the things that you have and can be thankful for the things that you desire as if you already have them, you'll attract more of what you're thankful for."

Thought Stopping - As mentioned earlier in this book you should constantly be vigilant of the thoughts and input you receive on a moment-to-moment basis. Whenever you find yourself the recipient of negative thoughts, words, vibrations or negativity in any form be sure to practice thought stopping. The rule of thumb is that it takes approximately 17 seconds for a thought to be activated in Source so if it's negative be sure to *stop and swap* it before then. On the other hand if it's a positive thought be sure to keep on thinking about it for at least 17 seconds or more.

Remove Temptation - Although this may seem an obvious step in creating a new habit it's still very important to mention. If there's anything within your influence that's a negative temptation or hindrance towards your goal, remove it. If for example you're in the process of creating a habit of being a non-smoker and you used to find yourself smoking most heavily while you were drinking in the local pub, you may want to eliminate frequenting the pub until after you've created your new habit. On a like manner if you're attempting to eat healthier you may want to take any chocolate bars or cake out of your refrigerator.

Create a Positive Environment - Make an immediate assessment of yourself, the people you associate with and your environment. Pay specific attention to listing anything or anyone that emanates negativity in your life. If there are any negative things in your environment, fix, replace, remove or eliminate them. If there are any negative people influencing your life you must also make the commitment to change, avoid or even remove yourself from their influence if at all possible. Negativity's the largest hindrance towards mental, spiritual or physical growth. Surround yourself with a positive environment as well as positive people.

Model Success - Is there anyone who has attained the goal that you're seeking after that you can model so as to also attain that goal? Remember, if anyone else has done it, so can you by following the same steps that they did. Success always leaves clues. The principle is by doing the exact same things that someone else has; you should be able to attain the exact same goals. If someone else has done it then it attainable.

How does it Help Me – What's the use of stepping outside of your comfort zone for a period of 30 days if there's no benefit in it for you? When you're creating your new habit, be sure that there's a clear and defined benefit for yourself. As often as you can during your 30 day process, reflect on these benefits and imagine yourself as having already attained them.

How does it Help Others – You've found by now through reading this book that one of the *keys to success* as well as the *purpose of the universe* is to give service. If you can place your goals in alignment with the goal of the universe you'll find much more strength in attaining them. As you're creating your goal think to yourself; "How will attaining this goal help others either directly or indirectly?"

* Do it Now - The main ingredient in getting anything done is *"action"*. How long are you going to think or simply dream of progressing? Remember, it's the nature of the conscious mind to remain within its comfort zone. It rebels against change even when the change is beneficial.

So it's imperative that as soon as you plan your goal or whatever habit it is you intend on attaining that you immediately take action. You may find it uncomfortable or inconvenient at first, which is simply your conscious mind rebelling against progress. This is also known as self-sabotage.

I promise you that if you continue in spite of this discomfort that within a very short time the discomfort will become less and will be replaced with a new drive to attain your goal. The difference between a successful person and a dreamer is action.

"Do it now!"

REMEMBER:

1. Creating a habit of the positive behavior or a goal is the key point that's required to maintain it permanently.

2. Any positive suggestion or change will be lost in 3 - 5 days for 85% of the public without repeated daily suggestion to create a permanent habit.

3. This habit creation formula is scientifically proven and will always work if followed properly.

4. You must follow the formula for a minimum of 30 days without missing a day.

5. You should create one new habit at a time.

6. Guided imagery and meditation are two of the most successful means of programming a new habit.

CHAPTER 8

PUTTING
IT
ALL TOGETHER

"Others can stop you temporarily.
You are the only one who can do it permanently."

Zig Ziglar

THIRTEEN STEP CHECKLIST

Read this entire book so you understand the following vital points before proceeding. If there is one point that you are not familiar with go to the chapter listed and refresh your memory.

- ☑ **1.** You have been programmed by your environment. More than 90% of your present life is being run by associations to past programs like a robot. *(Chapter 1)*
- ☑ **2.** The conscious mind is naturally rebellious to change and will try to stop your progress. *(Chapter 2)*
- ☑ **3.** The subconscious mind will *always* deliver what the conscious mind focuses on whether it's positive or negative. *(Chapter 2)*
- ☑ **4.** Practice "elite thought" rather than appearance or environmental thinking. *(Chapter 3)*
- ☑ **5.** Always take 100% responsibility for your life. *(Chapter 4)*
- ☑ **6.** The Superconscious mind is the connection between thought and Source energy. Any thought placed in this substance attracts similar frequencies to it. *(Chapter 5)*
- ☑ **7.** Find time to relax each day for health and higher, original thinking *(Chapter 5)*
- ☑ **8.** Choose your goal and place your order. *(Chapter 6)*
- ☑ **9.** Act as if you've already attained your goal. *(Chapter 6)*
- ☑ **10.** Your success is in direct proportion to your service and gratitude. *(Chapter 6)*
- ☑ **11.** The habit creating process is a biologically sound formula and will always work if you follow the process. *(Chapter 7)*
- ☑ **12.** Utilize a relaxation technique in the next section of this book to program yourself with the new habit. *(Chapter 8)*
- ☑ **13.** Never give up. Do it now!

RELAXATION TECHNIQUES FOR PROGRAMMING

To **Create your Permanent Habit / Goal** you'll want to imagine yourself being successful in whatever your goal happens to be. One of the most successful ways to do that is to use one of the following relaxation techniques to slow your mind and enter the Alpha Brainwave State.

Remember the subconscious mind sees imagined memories and actual memories as equal. So your new imagined memories will soon become engrained in your subconscious mind as your new habit or program. This will permanently replace any old or pre-existing negative habit.

In today's busy hustle and bustle many people find it nearly impossible to take even 10 to 15 minutes for themselves. It's very important that you do so. Find some time each day that you can take approximately 15 minutes for yourself. In these 15 minutes find a quiet place that you can relax where you'll not be interrupted. You don't necessarily have to meditate however take some time to let your mind relax and just let your mind roam free. You'll be surprised at the things that come to you when you take the time to quiet your mind.

Almost every self-help program you see today suggests that you take some time out of each day to quietly reflect or meditate. Before you run out to rent your own personal Monk to teach you how to do it, take a few moments to read this section. Meditation isn't the only option. There are many other alternatives to meditation such as guided imagery, hypnosis, daydreaming, prayer or simply sitting quietly without doing anything for 10 - 15 minutes.

HOW TO QUIET YOUR MIND EACH DAY

Reflection time gets you to slow down a bit so you can step back and take an objective look at yourself. As mentioned earlier in this book, most people are too busy living their lives to actually take the time to improve their lives. How would you know what to improve-on if you haven't looked at yourself to see if there's improvement required? It's like the woman who gets dressed in a hurry because she's late for work. She didn't have the time to take a look at herself before leaving home and all day long people were quietly laughing at her behind her back because she had two different colored shoes on. We live our lives the same way.

*"Observe your life and
your goals on a daily basis."*

Many years ago I used to meditate at a Buddhist Monastery in New Hampshire. Up to that point I thought that everything was fine in my life and was the way it should be. One day while I'd been meditating for a while I suddenly had a moment of enlightenment that was so intense that I opened my eyes in shock of the impressions I'd just received. I had a strong visualization of my life. It was as if I were on the outside as an observer looking in. The interesting thing is that I didn't like what I saw. I didn't like the person I'd become. I realized that I had become excessively conditioned by the propaganda of society and religion and especially the expectations of others. I barely recognized this mindless drone that was going through the numbers conducting the routines of his life. I was like a rat in a maze. What had happened to my powers of observation? Why did I not see what others saw? It was quite an eye opener. Since I didn't like what I saw, I changed it! I took control of my life; made the proper plans to get on track and instituted them immediately. That's where my life seemed to begin. It was a rebirth of sorts.

Meditation or some form of contemplation is important as a way to communicate with your inner self. In those quiet times your mind slows down which opens you up to the spiritual realm. In many of our training seminars we have the opportunity to work in the various brainwave states. Here's something very interesting I found; simply by closing your eyes you block out 80% of Beta Activity. That means you immediately enter 80% into the Alpha state. Why is that important? Alpha is the best state to be open to suggestion and perform any of the various relaxation techniques we're speaking of. Now if you combine your eye closing with taking three deep breaths and just letting go... then you'll find yourself right where you want to be.

"When your eyes close on the CONSCIOUS side,
they open on the SUBCONSCIOUS side."

MEDITATION

So as you close your eyes and enter this light meditative state simply allow your imagination to focus on the various things you're working on and be aware of your thoughts and emotions as you do. Welcome to the wonderful world of meditation.

There are many forms of meditation that you can practice. The main purpose is to slow down and relax. If you want to learn the formal approaches to meditation you can find many books on it in any bookstore. My goal here's to teach you the easy way or quick-guide to meditation so you can reap its benefits now.

The key feature of most of them seems to be to focus on only one thing at a time. In your normal Beta (waking, busy) State your mind's focused on many things simultaneously. Even as you're reading this book you're in Beta and are probably also thinking many other thoughts. You may be thinking about what's for dinner, what you're going to do this weekend, the weather outside, what the kids are doing

right now, I really need to clean my desk off and the thoughts go on…
It's very hard to relax with this inexhaustible thought machine running
at full throttle. Focusing on only one thing brings you to a relaxed state
that lets go of the outside world. Your mind will automatically begin to
slow down and as you slow down your Beta activity will become less
and you'll begin to slip into Alpha and possibly even the deeper states.
Don't worry about the deeper states however. Alpha's the best place
for programming your new habits.

Here are some of the focal points that you can use:
A candle flame
A statue of something peaceful
A spot on the wall slightly above eye level *(makes eyes tired)*
Your breathing, with your eyes opened
Your breathing, with your eyes closed

I prefer focusing on my breathing with my eyes closed for two reasons.

1. The act of simply closing your eyes shuts out the Beta activity
and automatically brings you into Alpha as mentioned earlier.

2. As a Buddhist Monk once explained to me; you can take your
breathing with you anywhere you go and not worry about
losing or forgetting it at home and if you don't have your
breathing anymore you really don't need to meditate either.

MEDITATIVE RELAXATION PROCESS

This is a non-denominational relaxation technique that I use that you
may find helpful. It's not a formal meditation so I'll call it meditative
relaxation. It can be used for programming your new goals into
permanent habits or simply as a means of relaxing each day to observe
your life and gain valuable insight.

Once you've decided upon your focal point, it's simply a matter of allowing your mind to focus on it without drifting. When I focus on my breathing I like to count each breath as it first begins up to 12 breaths and then begin the cycle over. If I happen to lose count or count over twelve breaths I simply start over again at number one. This is how I'm able to let go of all other thoughts. You can't do both and be successful. Once I'm able to count 3 – 4 complete sets of twelve, without distraction, I'm then ready to begin my imagination training or contemplating on my life depending on the purpose for my session.

QUIET REFLECTION

This can be a great, simple way to quiet your mind which is similar to the Meditative Relaxation without the format of counting breaths. The problem lies in being able to keep your mind free of the happenings of the day without having a focal point to help you. If you're able to relax this way without being distracted it may be the right option for you. Remember, the purpose is to step away from your busy day and allow your mind to enter the slower relaxing brainwave states.

> **THOUGHTS:** Another way to reflect quietly is to play meditative or classical music in the background. It will give you something to focus on that will help you to let go and relax. Be sure to use music that doesn't have words or sudden bursts of sound that will startle or distract you.

GUIDED IMAGERY

This is probably the simplest and my favorite way of letting go and allowing the programming to begin. It works just like it sounds. You are guided by an external voice or narrator to relax you and take you to the Alpha brainwave state. Once you're relaxed you simply allow the voice to guide you through the process of imagining yourself as being the goal you. Imagining you as already having accomplished the task or goal you're desirous to achieve. This type of guided imagery session is advantageous as it's preplanned and can include many features you wouldn't remember to include if you were doing it live or on the spot.

You can pre record a guided imagery session yourself or get one from us as we have them available at our website at: www.ChooseHypnosis.com/store.htm. We have various titles that can be used as well as wonderful generic ones that work for multiple issues. In addition to utilizing your imagination they'll also instill emotions and confidence so you can get the most out of them. If you're creating your own, keep in mind that it only needs to be 10 - 15 minutes tops. It's important to listen to the guided imagery session each day for 30 days without changing the topic you've chosen until it's complete. You can listen to them with your eyes opened or closed but obviously closed is more effective.

HYPNOSIS

Hypnosis has always been a great conditioning tool to create new behaviors and replace old ones. While participating in live hypnosis sessions is probably the most effective process for creating your desired change, it can be quite expensive to do it for 30 days in a row. An alternative to this would be to attend 4 sessions, once a week while listening to your guided imagery session on the in between days. Another alternative is to be hypnotized through telephone sessions which are just as effective and possibly even more effective if conducted properly. For a listing of qualified Hypnosis Practitioners, go to www.ChooseHypnosis.com.

SELF HYPNOSIS

Self Hypnosis is also a very powerful tool for self-help. It's very similar to the Guided Imagery process on the previous page. Keep in mind that all hypnosis or suggestibility is self-hypnosis as well. Whether you're giving or receiving suggestion, you're still hearing and accepting them unless you're actively resisting them. That's just the way it works. Your mind absorbs all information it comes in contact with. There are many great self-hypnosis books available. The best one I would suggest is THE EVERYTHING SELF-HYPNOSIS BOOK by Rene Bastarache. *(I just really like the author.)* You can find it in virtually any brick and mortar or online bookstore.

DAY DREAMING

I'm sure you're all familiar with this one. You may have been doing several times while reading this book, but I certainly hope not. Although daydreaming doesn't really have a focal point and is just letting your mind roam free it's still better for you than not doing any relaxing at all. Taking 20 - 30 minutes each day to simply sit and daydream can do wonders for your health and general demeanor. While you're at it let your mind daydream about what it would be like to have attained your goal.

PRAYER

Prayer is an often-misunderstood tool that can be used very effectively if done properly. Unfortunately as I just mentioned, it's often misunderstood. The concept of prayer is about speaking to or having a conversation with God / Source or whatever Higher Power is applicable to you. Most religions that use prayer are usually speaking to a deity they relate to as their Father or Creator.

Here's the issue. How would you speak to your *mortal father* when you need something or someone to talk to?

- Would you chant to him the same sentence over and over?

- Would you recite the same pre-written paragraphs over and over 40 to 50 times while holding beads so you don't lose your place?

- Would you speak really fast blurting out what you want and run away?

- Or would you speak to him?

Of course you'd speak to him if you wanted him to listen to you and once you spoke to him and asked him what you wanted you'd also stick around a few minutes to hear his response and see if he had something to say to you. After all; us fathers would like to speak with our children rather than be spoken to and then shoved off.

That's also how your prayers should be. When you're using prayer to attain a goal or replace a habit, take the time to speak to your Father and ask his help. While you're there take a little time to say hello, ask how he is and actually care to hear his answer. Don't just say hi, ask for money and run. No Father wants to hear that. Tell him how you're doing and what's really going on in your life. Let him know who you are and what makes you tick.

Tell him what you want, why you want it and what you expect to do with it. If it's replacing a bad habit, tell him why you want the new behavior and how it can help you and others once it is developed. Do you see where I'm going with this? If he's your Heavenly Father, he'll want to speak with you even more that your mortal father does. Take your time, be sincere and speak with him rather than at him.

THOUGHTS: At times people have a tendency to take Deity for granted. Remember the words of the late *Golden Rule Jones*, "Do to others what you'd like done to you." Repetitive prayers, chants and other people's prayers while they may be very eloquent and even historic won't give you what you want as they're not from you. Be original and speak from "your" heart.

MIGHTY PRAYER

If you really want to be effective while using prayer here's another way you can approach it. It's called "Mighty Prayer". I'll warn you first that this isn't for the faint of heart. It takes a true commitment but if you can do it the rewards will be equally great. The next time you kneel or sit to pray, once you begin, continue praying for a minimum of one hour. In that hour it's important to continually be speaking. I don't mean speaking incoherently as if you were in a race but not to let 2 – 3 minute gaps go by. The purpose isn't to sit quietly waiting but to get everything out of you that you have to say and then even more. If you're able to do that easily, then make it two hours the next time. Set your alarm clock so you're not distracted by checking your watch to see if time is up yet.

Here's what happens… In the first couple minutes you say hi, I want this, I want that, I'm okay, I like work and all the small talk. In the next 3 -5 minutes, you're kind of fidgeting thinking about what else to say. Then you get a little below the surface conversation and begin talking like you're talking to a real person about what's going on in your life. About 10 minutes goes by with more fidgeting, humming in your brain and wondering what to say next. Finally something happens and you find yourself bearing your soul and saying what really concerns you and makes you tick. You've finally truly opened up and are speaking to your Father about what really matters in your life. This is the point of Mighty Prayer. This is the point of life changing inspiration and enlightenment. Try it just once and see what happens.

SLEEP YOUR WAY TO SUCCESS

Let's face it. You go to sleep every night. So why not use that to your advantage? There's a way to use sleep to enhance your progress in attaining your goals. By the way, it doesn't involve having to sleep with anyone else either. This is a solo activity that will make a huge difference once you begin utilizing it.

Sleep conditioning is also an exceptional tool for growth as well as to attain your goals. The process of sleep conditioning constitutes going to sleep at night and just before you do keeping your most important thoughts in your mind by repeating them over and over like a mantra until you fall asleep. As you become tired you may stumble on the words or even forget them altogether so the most important thing to do as you're repeating the words is to *imagine* yourself having accomplished the goal that you're repeating. Your imagination is the key factor.

What's happening is the last thoughts you have when you go to sleep continue working in your subconscious mind as you're sleeping. From your subconscious mind it expands out into the superconscious that's also known as the universal subconscious. Of course now you know that you have a lot more going here than simply your own mind working on your goal as the superconscious and Source Energy are one and the same.

Many times while utilizing this sleep conditioning I've woken-up in the morning with the answers I was seeking. In fact there've been quite a few times that upon waking up I had such complete answers in my mind that I immediately walked into my office and filled up three entire dry erase boards before I finally exhausted all the information. That's the difference between waking up with a normal answer compared to a superconscious response. When the response you receive comes from the superconscious mind it will be complete and detailed.

GUIDED IMAGERY SCRIPT

Here's a script that you can record and listen to that will help you to program your new habit or goal each day. If you play relaxing music at the same time it will help to lessen outside distractions while listening to it.

Before you begin listening to this session be sure that you give yourself enough uninterrupted time to sit and listen to it quietly for at least 10 – 15 minutes. This session is designed to be listened to while relaxing. Don't listen to it while driving a motor vehicle or doing anything else that may be dangerous. Turn off any beepers or phones, including cell phones. Put any pets outside of the room that you're in if they may jump on your lap and disturb you. Now sit in a comfortable out of the way seat supporting your neck and back preferably. Be sure that there's nothing else in the area that may disturb you during your session.

When recording this script be sure to read it slowly and pause each time you see the three dots ... That will give you the time necessary to use your imagination.

NOTE: *One of the greatest benefits of this program is that it will work just as successfully whether you relax a lot, a little or not at all. The main purpose is to use your imagination as a way to create new memories. The subconscious mind cannot differentiate between an imagine memory or an actual memory. Therefore whether you relax deeply or simply listen to the instructions to imagine the scenes the same purpose is being accomplished.*

You Are The Creator
By Rene Bastarache, CI

(Record starting here)

Close your eyes and relax. Take a deep breath ... and exhale ... and take a second deep breath ... and exhale and on you third deep breath, hold it for about three seconds ... and exhale and relax.

Relax, every part of your body starting from the top of your head al the way down to the bottom of your feet...

In just a moment I'm going to count from 20 down to 1 ... and as I say each number I'd like you to imagine the number, think about it and quietly spell the number to yourself which will help you to deepen you own relaxation.

So let's begin with 20 as you spell it ... t-w-e-n-t-y ...19 ... n-i-n-e t-e-e-n ... 18 ... All the way down deep ... 17... 16... deeper and deeper ...15 ... keep on spelling the numbers to yourself quietly ... 14... just l yourself go... 13... 12 ... give yourself the permission that this is what you want to do ...11 ... 10... allow yourself to just let go ... 9 ... 8 ... deeper and deeper ... 7 ... 6 ... all the way down deep ... 5 ... 4 ... tired and drowsy ... 3 ... 2 ... so very relaxed ... and finally ...1 ... deep ... deep ... relaxation.

(On stage creation)

I'd like you to use your imagination right now. Imagine, or just think about, yourself sitting comfortably in front of a large movie screen and imagine that you're seeing a motion picture of yourself. See it as vividly and in as much detail as possible. See yourself in this motion picture reacting successfully, in the ideal situation, having already have attained your goal ... (pause) As you're imagining yourself as this successful person ... (pause) imagine yourself as the main actor or lead person on your screen ...

How do you "feel" now that you've become the person that you'd like to be ... (pause) ... Feel the emotions ... What would you be feeling ... What are you "feeling"? Maybe confidence ... pride ... fulfillment ... satisfaction ... relief ... happiness ... (pause) ... What emotions are you feeling exactly ... Let those emotions fill you up ... (pause) ... Let them grow within you ... (pause) ... What are you "hearing" associated with your new goal? What are others maybe saying about you? How do they feel about your accomplishments? ... (pause) ...

I'd also like you to imagine and feel what you think is different ... What's different now that you've attained your goal? How has your life changed? ... (pause) ... Are you enjoying any more freedoms associated with this attainment? ... Think about them... get them clearly in your mind as you visualize yourself standing in front of you... on that motion picture screen. ... (pause) ... See the details ... What are you wearing? ... What are you doing? ... What else is there that you can notice that is associated with this now orderly achievement? ... (pause)

Remember the imagining of yourself doing something with enough detail is equal to the actual experience as far as your subconscious mind is concerned... So, see yourself for just a few more moments having achieved your new habit. ... (pause) ...

(Old habit is GONE)

You're in control of your life now ... You have created and attained a new positive habit ... With the power of your subconscious mind, it's very easy to do ... You've allowed the past disorder to fade away like an unwanted memory ... and now you move forward ... The disorder of the past has been replaced with order. The dysfunctionality replaced with functionality. So once again feel that wonderful sense of satisfaction and achievement. It's coming from that strong subconscious mind that you have. You've created your goal and through these daily exercises maintaining it, creating a permanent habit of change.

(Awakening III)

At the count of five you'll come back to the here and now, feeling wonderful in every way ... One ... Beginning to come all the way back, Two ... Coming back feeling better and better, Three ... Feeling totally relaxed and comfortable, Four ... Eyes starting to open now... and, Five Eyes wide open, feeling wonderful in every way.

REMEMBER:

1. Choose the form of relaxation you'd like to use to begin programming your habit.

2. Guided imagery or meditation can be helpful as they're able to guide you through the instructions and you simply listen and imagine.

3. You can also create your own guided imagery by recording the script included in this chapter and then listening to it daily for 30 days.

4. You must see yourself as "already" having accomplished the task you are working towards. Always see the end results.

5. Even if you don't have a goal or habit to create; quiet meditation, contemplation or prayer is still very helpful in creating health, abundance and happiness. They help you to see outside the box and create direction in your life.

HOW TO SUCCEED

* Study this book.
* Carry it with you.
* Do the exercises. Write in it.
* Help others by teaching them what you've learned.
* Make a decision to do it now!
* Grow - stretch - do what's uncomfortable.
* Reach for more than is normal.
* Do what you have NOT done before.
* Stop being a victim by taking 100% responsibility for your life.
* Most importantly ... Make a Choice!

   If you don't, one will be made for you.

* NOTE: Choosing not to act is also a choice.

HOW NOT TO SUCCEED

- Put this book back on the shelf.
- Do what's comfortable.
- Decide to get back to it later on.
- Don't take responsibility for your life.
- Remain a victim of your circumstances.
- Do the same things you've been doing - nothing new!

> *"In order to change, there must be a change!"*
> *"How much do you really want to succeed?"*

Remember, the key to success is repetition and perseverance. You must keep with it. We'd like to leave you with this parting thought,

13AUTHORS PARTING THOUGHTS

If your financial, health or relationship status were lacking in some way when you first received this book; understand that it wasn't your fault. You didn't know how to improve it and you didn't have the tools necessary at that time.

If you're not able to succeed in your goals now however; it is your fault! You have been given the knowledge and are holding the instruction manual in your hands. Use it!

If you need further assistance with your growth or would like to attend a live group seminar with others of like interest, contact us. Our seminars are designed to give you the jump-start you may need and in a short time you'll be on your fast track to success. You'll just need to keep the momentum going.

"It's never too late to begin a positive change in your life."

We'd like to thank you for the opportunity for letting us make a difference in yours.

"Be Happy!"

Rene & Raluca

P.S. Drop us a line and let us know about your success.
Visit us online for Seminars, Corporate Training and Self Help Tools.
admin@ChooseHypnosis.com
www.ChooseHypnosis.com
AmericanSchoolofHypnosis.com

THE END

For real this time

FREE RESOURCES

Learn Hypnosis FREE - (447 page book) - To learn more about suggestibility, programming, self-help and changing the lives of yourself and others, download our amazing manual "Clinical Hypnosis Training Manual form A- Z", FREE at http://www.choosehypnosis.com Consider this gift as our business card. Study it, try it and make an informed decision is if this is the path for your self-discovery without spending a dime.

Enjoy the book and if nothing else I guarantee it will change the way you look at life. For the better!

ADDITIONAL RECOURCES

Here's more products created by Rene & Raluca:
Over thirty-five self-help books and manuals
Over twenty-five home study and live certification courses
Over fifty self-help mp3complete conditioning audio sessions
Go to: http://www.choosehypnosis.com/store.htm

Made in the USA
Las Vegas, NV
02 November 2021